COUNTRY CAPERS

by Ken Dykes

cover design by Wendy Dykes

© 2013 Ken Dykes. All rights reserved.

To Tim and Penny, hoping their childhood was as exciting and enjoyable as my own.

ACKNOWLEDGEMENTS: My thanks are extended to all family, friends and acquaintances mentioned in this book.

Without their very existence the telling of my story would not have been possible.

To my friends and relatives in America, my apologies for the sometimes (to them) peculiar spellings!

CONTENTS.

FOREWORD

COUNTRY CAPERS is an autobiographical account of a youngster growing up in the English countryside during and just after the Second World War.

During those dark days, when almost everything was rationed, we were usually hungry (in fact we were always hungry) and the majority of our 'country capers' involved schemes aimed at increasing our calorie intake.

Home entertainment consisted of the radio. There was no children's television. In fact there was no television at all, that came later, so most of our pleasures were pursued outdoors.

When not at school we spent virtually every daylight hour, summer and winter, rain or shine, out in the woods, over the fields, across the moors or searching the river bank. During the summer holidays we would literally disappear all day, building dens and tree houses or foraging for anything we could find to eat.

We, that is to say, the little band of five or six like-aged friends, saw very few other people during our forays in the countryside.

Farms were much smaller then and if they didn't have a dairy herd they at least had a few milk cows so that at three o'clock every afternoon we knew the farmer and his workers would be in the cowshed, milking. At such times we were free to roam the deserted fields.

At other times of the day they would all be out in those same fields, doing the things that farmers do with tractors in fields. We were then free to roam the deserted farm yards!

On reflection, there were some days when we weren't so hungry. School dinners. Our village school had no kitchen or dining hall so we had to 'crocodile', in pairs, the half mile down the road to the village hall every day where a small band of dedicated ladies prepared the meals.

I loved them (school dinners, that is, not the dinner ladies). They were not large but they were delicious. And I don't recall there being a national problem with obesity.

Many of our rural pursuits would not then have been considered too unusual (most other people were doing the same).

Today, however, some of our activities would be very much frowned upon—and the rest are downright illegal!

Ken Dykes

(Contains some mild expletives).

1: MOVING TARGET.

TO enjoy the privilege of growing up in the English countryside is a favour bestowed by circumstance, usually of birth.

In my own case I should, by rights, have been a "townie" but my destiny was reshaped at an early age by a certain Austrian gentleman.

Adolf Hitler.

As far as I am aware he was not exactly in the habit of lending anything like a helping hand to anyone and, to my knowledge at least, did precious little of benefit to anyone.

The favour he did me was, I feel certain, purely unintentional.

Anyway, it was one of Herr Hitler's bombs which in 1940 reduced our house, in a normally quiet Hampshire market town, to rubble while we—or rather the grown-ups as I was only four years old at the time—sang "Ten Green Bottles" in the frightening half-dark of an underground air raid shelter at the end of our little cul-de-sac street.

That song, its verses punctuated by the "crump" of high explosives, was to be indelibly imprinted on my young mind.

Homeless ("bombed out" seemed to be the unofficial terminology) we went to live "temporarily" with relatives in the village of Old Basing, three miles away.

It was an evacuation that, fortunately for me, was to last not only for the rest of the war but the rest of my childhood and early adult life as well.

It soon became apparent, however, that despite our move into the relative safety of the country, Mr Hitler had not abandoned his seemingly strategic plan to exterminate me, or even to allow the family to enjoy the new-found pleasures of life in a sleepy village.

After a few weeks "camping-out" with Aunt Lil, we moved across the lane into an empty estate cottage. But only to find that we were, once again, the target for a hit and run raid by a German bomber. The far-off wailing of the air raid siren, rising and falling mournfully to signify the approach of enemy aircraft, sounded distinctly eerie, even in broad daylight, and sent a tingle racing up the spine to stimulate the hairs at the back of the neck into involuntary motion.

The sound also sent us, that is me and Mum, (Dad was at work and older brother John was at school) scurrying through the hedge in terror to seek shelter under Floss Long's stairs.

Hiding under the stairs was officially accepted as being the safest place to be during an air raid for those who had no underground shelter.

Strictly speaking we should have sheltered under our own stairs. But our under-stair cupboard was so dark and dusty that I believe my mother would rather have braved Hitler's bombs than the possibility of an encounter with one of the huge hairy spiders known to lurk there.

So under the neighbour's stairs we crouched, hands in ears, as once again the crunch of German bombs echoed around.

The long and baleful single note of the siren's "all clear" eventually came faintly through and we emerged from the tiny cupboard shaking but unhurt.

A cup of tea all round seemed to be all that was needed to make everything right as ninepence again while the sudden flood of chatter, in stark contrast to the silence under the stairs, relieved the tension.

Later, back at the cottage, the family was settling down to tea when there was a knock at the door.

Actually that's a slight understatement. It was more of a thunderous hammering.

Dad opened the door.

'Sorry', yelled a very red-faced man in a tin hat. 'You've got to get out. Quick. Unexploded bomb. Mr Angel's garden!'

As Mr Angel lived no more than twenty-five or thirty yards away we needed little urging. Mother threw some things into a bag and we trooped out.

Herr Hitler had done it again.This time we walked the mile or so down the hill, and over the River Loddon bridge, to grandfather's house where, after finishing our interrupted tea, and spending a good deal of time talking about the day's events, we all went to bed on spare chairs and sofas.

It was another two days before the bomb disposal men actually disposed of the rogue bomb but it was two more days of gran's baking skills before, almost reluctantly, we marched back home.

That was not to be my last encounter with the weaponry of the Third Reich. Hitler, it seemed, was determined to eliminate me. His spies must have been everywhere.

My next escape, however, was not from a German threat but from the very Allies who were supposed to be on our side, fighting the Nazis.

It was two years later.

One morning I was leaning over the brick parapet of the river bridge already mentioned, studying a big trout which was just visible in the water below, beneath one of the arches

It looked so temptingly close. Even at the age of six I was beginning to get the irresistible poaching urge that would return to haunt me again and again.

And I was trying to figure out a way of getting that fish out of the river and on to a plate.

In the distance I became aware, almost subconsciously, of a low rumbling sound which, as it drew nearer, seemed to be accompanied by a peculiar metallic rattling and clanking.

Into view at last came an armoured personnel carrier on tracks with a little round turret affair on the top in which sat a very superior looking military man wearing headphones.

The little crowd of children chasing the machine on foot, on trike and on bike, indicated that it was almost certainly owned by Canadians, or possible newly-arrived Americans, both of whom had the most delightful habit of chucking packets of chewing gum, and sometimes even chocolate, to any well-wisher, especially children.

My first reaction was to join the pursuit but it quickly became apparent that, with a dozen or so kids already in the race, many of them bigger than me, my chances of collecting any goodies at all were pretty slim.

Always one to conserve energy whenever possible, I decided to give it a miss.

The carrier came rumbling on towards me as I leaned against the brickwork of the bridge, the noise of its progress gradually growing to a deafening din.

As the bridge was narrow I moved off to a wider part of the road to wait for it to pass.

With a certain exciting fascination I watched in some awe as the clanking giant passed me and started to climb the little rise over the bridge, the metal tracks making an odd echoing sound as the vehicle began to cross. The soldier in the turret, meanwhile, sat rigidly upright, looking neither to left nor right.

Then, with dramatic suddenness, the metal monstrosity slewed around in the very centre of the bridge, the tracks sending out showers of sparks and gouging deep score marks into the surface of the road.

It turned a full ninety degrees to the right and smashed into the brick parapet at the very spot where, a few moments before, I had been hanging over the top, gazing into the river.

A ten-feet long section of the brickwork split, toppled, and crashed into the water below.

The carrier, still moving, inched forward into the gap the fallen bricks had left in the wall. The great machine came almost to a halt, teetered for a second or so on the very edge of the roadway, then, it seemed in slow motion, toppled forward and, amid the screams and shouts of 'Look out!'

and 'B-loody hell!' from a dozen young voices, fell with an almighty splash upside-down in the river.

The soldier on the top, who had scrambled up out of the turret, crouched on hands and knees on the back of the monster as it crashed through the bridge. Then, as it fell, he leapt outwards and forwards into the water, by great good fortune clear of its crushing weight.

A whole crowd of us stood, dumbfounded, gazing at the upturned belly of the carrier, now emitting clouds of steam and smoke, sticking up above the surface.

The river was no more than about three feet deep and the soldier who had jumped clear came wading out, dripping water but otherwise unhurt. The only other occupant, the driver, was still trapped inside.

Within minutes, it seemed, there were swarms of military personnel on the scene, armed with all manner of fascinating cutting and lifting gear.

Even so it took rescuers an hour or more to free the driver, happily suffering nothing worse than a broken arm, the water being too shallow to cover him.

The recovery teams were all day hoisting the carrier out of the river and back onto the road. Then they carted it off on a big transporter for repairs. But the whole episode gave us something to watch for hours—and talk about for years.

I had more reason to talk about it , and remember it, than anyone but if I had thought that this adventure was to be my last brush with the military I should have been sadly mistaken. In fact my next encounter was to result in my one and only war wound.

Some Canadian troops had temporarily taken over a large area of parkland that surrounded the Civil War ruin of Basing House at the edge of the village.

All that remained of the castle itself was a vast pile of devastated brickwork, it was truly "one of the ruins that Cromwell knocked about a bit". But the fifty acres or so of grounds had been transformed into a massive army campsite.

The soldiers were billeted there for some weeks before moving off towards the south coast for embarkation to theatres of war in various parts of the world and it didn't take us long to discover that all kinds of goodies could be scrounged from these big-hearted lads.

On my only lone visit to the camp I rode my old tricycle. I was too big for it really but it was the only transport I possessed and home was a mile and a half away.

Turning off the village Street, as it was grandly named, I pedalled up the steep gravelled driveway, under the ruined arch of the garrison gateway, over the canal bridge and round the bend at the top, on up into the camp.

It was a long, hard climb on a little trike and I had to stand up on the pedals to keep moving. By the time I reached the top I was blowing like an out-of-condition porpoise.

Once in the camp I wandered around (security, it seemed, was non-existent) gazing at the tents, camp kitchens and piles of equipment.

At length I paused beside a tent where some cooking activity was in progress. A soldier in khaki trousers and shirt, the sleeves rolled up to the elbows, was frying something in a big blackened pan over an open camp stove.

I stood and watched.

The man in khaki glanced up, then, without a word, lowered his head again and got on with his cooking.

I continued to watch.

He glanced up again.

Finally he dug into the pan with a fork and held up a smoking hot slice of fried bread.

'Want this, son?' he drawled.

'Please!'

A slice of fried bread doesn't sound like much, nor very exciting, now. But in those dark days of rationing and shortages, free food was free food—and even a slice of fried bread was more than welcome to an ever-hungry young tummy.

With a grin on his face he held it out to me.

I took it gingerly off the fork, holding it carefully between forefinger and thumb

The grin on the soldier's face widened as I changed hands, dropped it back into the palm of the first hand, then back again, and again, until it cooled sufficiently to hold in comfort.

'All right, son?'

'Yeah!!'

And the soldier and his mates all laughed at the look of sheer delight that lit up my face.

With something approaching elation I inspected my prize as the soldier and his friends busied themselves about more cooking.

I found I had a piece of prime fried bread, cooked a golden brown, crisp, and not too greasy.

Lovely grub!

I pushed it up the front of my tight fitting, little-bit-too-small, green woollen jumper, hopped on my trike and headed for home.

This was something I was really going to enjoy.

Excitement must have got the better of me. I pedalled hard down the path from the camp, onto the gravel drive, round the corner at the top of the steep slope and over the canal bridge. It was then I remembered that the only braking system on the trike was the little lever operating two rubber brake blocks on the rim of the front wheel. And the lever was broken.

I was already on the slope and gathering speed down towards the main road. The trike was going too fast. Much too fast. And if I jumped off now that gravel would play havoc with my knees, elbows and face.

It was as much as I could do to keep the machine upright and straight as it bumped and bounced its way down the hill, gathering more speed all the while.

We flashed under the ruined archway, faster still, and careered towards the road. I shut my eyes.

Luckily there was nothing in the way of traffic passing on the road, not altogether surprising as vehicles of any kind were a good deal fewer and farther between in those days,

The trike, with me on board, clinging on tight and with legs outstretched in a vain effort to slow it down, hurtled straight across the road and smashed full tilt into the low stone wall on the other side.

Then everything went blank.

When I came to I was lying in someone's front garden flower bed among the crushed remains of the bedding plants.

I got shakily to my feet and peered over the wall.

My trike was lying in the road. It was a write-off. The front forks were bent back, the front wheel buckled into a sort of a figure-of-eight, the handlebars faced crazily sideways and the frame itself looked a good foot shorter than before.

I stood in a daze, staring at the wreckage of my poor trike, my feet still in the devastated flower border. Then I became aware of something wet and warm running down my neck. I wiped my neck with the back of my hand and looked aghast as I realised that the warm wetness was blood. My blood.

'Oohh!' I moaned. Suddenly I felt very weak.

There was a gash on my chin where I'd hit the top of wall as I sailed over. Blood was streaming down my jumper and trousers,

Then someone, presumably the lady in whose garden I had just crash-landed, appeared like a ministering angel and began to dab my injured chin with a piece of damp white rag.

How I eventually got home is still a bit hazy. I seem to recall an uncle—of which I had several living in the village—arriving to carry me off in his arms. At home my mother managed to staunch the flow of blood from my chin and started to remove my blood-soaked clothing.

As my jumper was peeled off over my head something fell to the floor.

'What's this?' asked my mother, holding up the object for me to see.

It was my lovely piece of fried bread. Only now it was cold, crushed and soaked in congealed blood.

I just burst into tears. And I carry the scar of my war wound on my chin to this day.

It was to be some months later that I suffered my most distressing war experience.

A crowd of us were engaged one afternoon in an impromptu game of cricket on the village playing field when someone shouted a warning.

Coming towards us, low and slow, was a single engined fighter plane. Smoke and flames billowed out behind it

'It's one of ours,' one keen young aero-expert declared. 'A Mustang'.

But that didn't alter the fact that it was obviously in serious trouble—and heading straight for our cricket pitch.

'Look out!' came a somehow familiar shout and we scattered.

From the comparative safety of the hedges on each side of the playing field we watched in awesome silence as the stricken plane, its engine spluttering and coughing, swept low over our erstwhile cricket pitch. We could clearly see the pilot at the controls.

The fighter cleared our field, and the village allotment gardens beyond, rose momentarily to miss the main railway line and telephone cables that ran along its bank, then plunged through the tops of the trees of a little wood two hundred yards away and nose-dived into the stubble field beyond.

There was a great roar as a frightening mass of vivid orange flames leapt into the air above the trees where the plane went down. A thick pall of black smoke mushroomed hundreds of feet into the sky. The crack and boom of exploding cannon shells echoed over the little wood.

By the time we had raced nearly half a mile up the track to the footbridge over the railway line and approached the scene the various services were arriving.

We were turned away and stood some way off to watch the figures milling about the flaming inferno.

Later, when the fire had been smothered and the pilot's body removed, we were allowed a bit closer.

The combined smell of burnt rubber, aero fuel, hot metal and melted perspex was overpowering. Lying on the blackened ground near the burned-out wreckage was a pitifully small piece of white parachute silk, charred at the edges.

So far my "peaceful life" in the country had been far from peaceful. And when I was just nine years old Herr Hitler made his final desperate attempt to finish me.

One sunlit morning, having been drawn as usual to the river, a group of us was standing on the bridge planning our day's curriculum. It was the same bridge which had so nearly been the scene of my demise in the earlier incident with the armoured carrier.

On this occasion our attention was suddenly focussed on a strange aircraft which seemed to be cruising noiselessly overhead. It was difficult to judge its exact height but to us it seemed to be very low.

Too low.

'What is it?' someone wanted to know.

'It's a Lockheed Lightning,' returned my big brother who, besides being the leader of our gang, considered himself the highest authority on the recognition of American war planes.

The craft banked to the right and dipped slightly as several pairs of eyes watched attentively.

That was when it became clear that what my brother had mistaken for the twin-boom fuselage of a Lightning was in fact a short squat body with a ram-jet mounted on the top. At the same time we saw the stubby squared-off wings that looked too small to keep the thing airborne.

My brother corrected himself. Hurriedly.

'No it's not. It's a bloody doodlebug.. Look out. Get down!'

This time he was right.

We hadn't heard the normally noisy ram-jet engine because it had already cut out and the flying bomb, Hitler's V-One, was now half falling, half gliding down to explode.

Along with the others I threw myself down behind the brick parapet of the bridge (workmen had already rebuilt the piece on the other side of the road where the carrier had gone through) and crouched, hands over ears but with eyes wide open, staring at the brickwork three inches in front of my nose.

The explosion, when it came, was terrifying.

The whole bridge shook and it flashed through my mind that it might collapse into the river with all of us on it. A shower of dust and small pieces of mortar fell in a kind of curtain down the wall just in front of my face and I remember the peculiar sight of the shock wave from the huge bang arching round the sky above me.

We rose slowly and shakily to our feet and peered over the top of the parapet.

Six or seven hundred yards away on a hill stood a farm. The flying bomb had come down almost beside the farmhouse which, despite having every pane of glass shattered and most of the tiles stripped from the roof by the blast, was, amazingly, still standing.

A dense cloud of black smoke plumed upwards as we headed for the scene. We had to cross three fields, negotiating hedges and ditches, to reach the spot and as we got closer passed numerous lumps of hot and twisted metal lying in the grass.

We approached the crater with awe.

A gaping hole ten feet deep and twenty feet across had appeared. We gazed down into the smoking depression. Of other parts of the V-One there was no sign.

Within a remarkably short time we were turned away from the scene by grown-ups who always had this infuriating habit of curbing our enthusiasm. So we had to be content with searching the surrounding fields for pieces of shrapnel small enough to carry.

Already a number of other kids were combing the area, bent on the same task.

What the doodlebug was doing in the heart of the Hampshire countryside, so far from its supposed target in the greater London area, had to remain a matter for some conjecture.

One theory was that its guidance system had been put out of action by an attack from an Allied fighter plane. And one of my friends found a piece of misshapen metal with a neat round hole punched through it which, he was adamant, had been made by a Spitfire's canon shell.

I was convinced, of course, that it was really just another attempt by the Fuhrer get rid of me. Why, I wondered, did he hold such a grudge against me?

Whatever the theory, the fact of the matter was that this was to be Adolf's last attempt on my young life.

A few weeks later he ended his own life in a Berlin bunker.

Once the most powerful man in Europe, the man who had brought misery and death to millions was finally found to be not brave enough to face the inevitable consequences that would follow the imminent defeat of the Third Reich by the Allies.

The conflict against Japan in the Far East was destined to drag on for several more months, costing thousands more lives, until cut short by the dropping of the world's first two nuclear bombs.

But the war in Europe had at last come to an end and I was left, finally, to settle down to an uneventful life of typical rural tranquillity in our quiet country home.

Or so I thought.

2: UP THE GARDEN PATH.

MOST people like to dream about their own idea of the perfect home and to many this means a cottage in the country with rambling roses growing all over the front porch and a garden full of old-fashioned flowers.

The dream is a pretty one, especially today with light at the flick of a switch, central heating, double glazing, water on tap and well-designed bathrooms.

The reality for those who actually lived in country cottages three or four generations ago was often somewhat harsher, as we found out when we moved from our bomb-damaged terraced town house into a village during the dark early days of World War Two.

It had been unoccupied, the cottage that is, for some years. There was dust and dirt everywhere and the only flowers in the garden were docks and thistles and dandelions. Even they had to struggle for survival among the beds of nettles and the long grass.

The cottage had no heating save the living room fire, no lighting but a single gas lamp, also in the living room (if you discount the candles), no bathroom, no mains water. Oh, and a visit to the lavatory meant a long walk outside.

We had a privy which stood in splendid isolation at the far end of the garden, against a broken down fence.

A winding, unkempt path, worn smooth by the passage of time and countless hurrying feet, meandered past what had once been a vegetable plot. It detoured two ancient apple trees that hadn't seen a pruning knife or a decent crop of fruit in years. Passed a rose bush that was as overgrown as a bramble and led, finally, through a big bed of stinging nettles, to the privy door.

When the weather was dry the path was dusty.

When the weather was wet the path was muddy.

In deepest winter it became either an icy slide or was completely obliterated by snow.

At such times one did not embark lightly on a trek up the garden path and we were often reminded of the question posed on those old war time railway posters: “Is your journey really necessary?”

The privy itself was built of overlapping horizontal planks, had a corrugated iron roof and was covered all over with a thick growth of ivy which, judging from the thickness of the stem, had been growing there almost as long as the privy had existed. In fact in my younger days, when I was small and light enough, on a warm day I would often climb the hairy trunk of the twisted creeper, clamber onto the roof and sit in majestic solemnity, surveying my domain.

The door was a solid wooden job with timber cross pieces on the back, not like the flimsy doors you get today, and was fastened by a rusty latch which sometimes held it shut and sometimes didn’t.

At the top of the door was a six-inch gap which let in a little daylight. At the bottom was a similar gap which let in a little more. Apart from this concession there was no light of any kind, not even a fancy shaped hole in the door. So at night, unless you didn’t mind groping your way out and then sitting in the dark, you had to make sure your torch batteries were in order.

Inside, the privy measured about four feet wide by six feet deep and the “seat” (it was more like a low work bench) spanned the width from wall to wall.

It was a grand seat.

As well as being four feet wide it was nearly three feet from front to back, a vast expanse of well-seasoned wood, bleached by generations of scrubbing brushes, and taking up almost half the total inside area of the privy.

The gaping black hole, nearer the front edge than the back, was almost circular and the rim of this aperture, which, certainly to a youngster, appeared to have enormous proportions, had been worn to such an extent by successive bottoms that the grain of the timber stood out in relief.

Here and there were little groups of woodworm holes, uninhabited I always assumed, as the occupants must have become extinct within a short time of the wood in which they had made their home being used for its present purpose.

The timber frame of the entire structure made the inside walls a jumble of uprights, cross pieces, tie pieces and runners, all unplaned and providing an endless and varied selection of corners and angles that were havens for dozens of spiders of all shapes and sizes, including the big hairy ones that have always turned my knees to jelly.

There was neither bolt nor lock on the door but by sitting forward on the front edge of the seat and stretching out a foot you could hold it closed with the toe of your shoe.

Conversely, as the door opened inwards, if the weather was clement your knee could hold it nicely open to let the sun shine in.

The floor was of brick.

A large nail had been driven into one of the uprights near your left elbow and to this was tied a length of string on which, normally, was threaded several dozen nine-inch squares of torn-up *News Chronicle.*

Sometimes this job had been neglected and there was just an old issue of the newspaper thrown down on the wide expanse of the seat for you to tear up yourself as and when required. At other times it might be one of those new glossy magazines, you know, the ones that leave sharp, hard ridges and corners when they're folded or crumpled.

Worst of all there were occasions when there was nothing at all, a fact that you never discovered until it was too late. Then you were in trouble.

In the front of the woodwork beneath the seat was a square door, like a cupboard door, held shut by two little metal swivel catches.

Open the door and inside was the bucket.

Its rim was slightly flared, after the fashion of a coal scuttle, and it had a hefty carrying handle, hinged on each side. There was a smaller steadying handle fixed to the back.

The bucket had to be emptied.

Often.

From the age of about twelve it became my responsibility to perform this duty, an honour I “inherited”, without a great deal of enthusiasm I might add, from my older brother.

But there it was, the job had to be done and part of my weekly pocket money depended upon my performing the ritual.

First you picked a spot in the garden, dug a hole as deep as you could (or, more often, as deep as you felt inclined) unfastened the catches on the little door, humped the bucket out to the hole and tipped it in, trying desperately not to spill it on your shoes.

You splashed a few drops of “Jeyes Fluid” into the bucket, swished it round a few times for good measure, replaced the bucket in the privy, then filled in the hole.

Easy.

Only, so many buckets had been emptied over the years in the more accessible parts of the garden that sometimes it was difficult to pick a spot that hadn’t been used too recently.

One thing though. All those years of bucket emptying enabled the garden to produce some of the finest vegetables in the village, once we’d got the garden down to cultivation, that is. Nowadays it’s known as “organic husbandry”.

Eventually I was relieved of this thoroughly irksome task by the local council’s introduction of a bucket emptying service.

Every week a large tanker lorry, painted rural green, pulled up at the cottage gate and down stepped a man clad in dark blue boiler suit, green wellington boots and thick red rubber gloves.

He carried a wide-topped bin-like container up our garden path, emptied our bucket into it and carried it back to the lorry.

Then he had to climb onto a step at the rear of the vehicle and tip the contents of his bin through a large hole into the murky depths of the lorry tank. He closed down the lid with a clang, hung his bin-bucket on a hook under the lorry and was ready to go.

You could always tell when the sewage lorry was coming, even more so that it had just been, as it left its own distinctive aroma wafting down the village street.

"Stink lorry" we used to call it. And it goes without saying that it had a few more colourful names as well.

One day I creosoted the privy inside and out. Made a fine job of it too. Even creosoted the seat.

That last little touch was a big mistake—as my younger sister, Sue, was to discover on using the privy soon after I'd finished the job, and before the dark brown, tarry application was properly dry.

Only total immersion in warm soapy water of that part of her anatomy affected, a vigorous scrubbing and liberal applications of calomine lotion finally stopped the stinging in her bottom.

I have never been forgiven.

And I was made to clean all the creosote off the seat as best I could before anyone else could use it.

In spite of the long, cold, wet treks up the garden, sometimes—when the need arose—at dead of night, having a privy did have certain compensations.

A wooden seat is, for some reason, never cold. And then, on a fine May morning, with the door propped open and the sun streaming in, you could sit in peaceful contemplation, seeing the little white patches of cloud gradually changing shape as they drifted across the blue of the sky, watching the antics of grasshoppers and other minutiae among the herbage near the door, or just listening to the pleasing sound of the call of a far-off cuckoo.

It was several years before we got proper "tap" water.

All our supplies, for washing, cooking, drinking and bathing, had to be fetched by bucket from the communal well nearby.

At first my mother fetched the water herself (dad was by this time driving a tank or something around the deserts of North Africa in pursuit of—or retreat from—Rommel the Desert Fox) but eventually my older brother and I were allowed the dubious pleasure of humping it home, although the job did have its own peculiar attractions.

Usual time for refilling the water bucket was straight after school in the afternoon. The well, thirty yards up the road from our front gate, had a heavy wooden flap, like a trap door, covering the gaping brick-lined hole.

This was to stop cats, dogs, hedgehogs, careless children and inebriated adults and suchlike from falling in.

It also stopped us from dropping stones down the well-shaft in order to count the seconds before the splash echoed back up from the depths. Even so, we did now and again find the opportunity to indulge in this exciting and satisfying pastime, much to the obvious disgust of the other well users.

How often did Mrs Manning fling open her cottage window across the road to yell her annoyance?

'Get away from that well, you little devils. Don't you know people have got to DRINK that water'

And we ran.

Over the well shaft was built a peculiar little lean-to shelter made of timber with a tiny ridged roof. Into this shelter was built the bucket winding gear.

A large wooden roller was slung between the two main uprights and on one end was fixed the handle, forged from a single length of heavy iron bar, protruding from the side of the well cover.

To this roller was attached a long length of thick chain, wound round and round the roller in several layers and to the free end of which was fixed one of those sprung, self-locking hooks that would hold the handle of the bucket.

The iron handle was worn smooth and shiny by constant use (at least half a dozen cottages still depended on the well for their water).

The chain itself, quite contrary to what you might expect, was rusty at the top end, the part that never went into the water, while the bottom few feet, those links that were constantly being immersed, were clean and shiny as new.

Where the links continually bit into the same position on the roller the wood was worn with an odd looking pattern of depressions, arranged in rings around its circumference.

The proper way to fill the bucket, as we were constantly being told by nosey neighbours, was to hook the chain to the bucket handle, steadying it so it didn't swing against the side of the well, and, using one hand as a brake on the roller, allow the weight of the bucket and chain to make a controlled descent down the well shaft.

The iron handle should rotate freely but slowly with your palm applying more and more drag on the roller as the combined weight of the bucket and unravelling chain increased.

However, we found it much more exhilarating to hook the bucket on, stand well clear, and heave the bucket into the well.

The weight of the metal bucket and the chain together set the whole thing plunging down the shaft, swinging and banging the side in a most exciting way as it went, increasing speed all the time.

The heavy iron handle became a lethal weapon as it spun wildly like the propeller of some strange aircraft.

As the roller rolled and the handle spun at breakneck speed the whole wooden structure, roof and all, rocked violently, at the same time issuing frightful rumbling sounds.

The action ended when the fast-falling bucket struck the surface of the water far below (it was a very deep well) with an enormous splash which echoed strangely back up to our appreciative ears.

Mrs Manning, and all the other well-users, weren't nearly so appreciative.

In fact they were outraged.

Normally the water that came out of that well was beautifully cool and crystal clear, sparkling almost. The best water I have ever tasted.

After the falling bucket trick the water wasn't so clear and not nearly as sparkling.

What happened was that with the winding gear running free and with the great weight of chain hurtling down the well, the whole lot sank straight to the bottom of the underground spring, stirring up centuries old deposits of mud, sand and gravel.

Anyone using the well within about half an hour of our visit got a decidedly murky bucketful.

Around would come the deputation, banging on the front door of our cottage.

'It's them boys of your'n again. Stirring up the well again. I've told 'em an' I've told 'em. You should see my water. Wanted a cup o' tea 'an all. Blah...blah...blah…'.

And mother would say she was sorry. That we'd gone out. But she would certainly give us what for when we came back.

As soon as they'd gone and were out of earshot she would come through to the kitchen, where we'd been hiding since the first bang on the door, and proceed to set about our legs with a damp, rolled up tea towel.

Though not very seriously.

Eventually the day dawned when two workmen turned up "from the estate" to "put on the water". They dug a trench from the roadway, then down the brick path at the side of the cottage, knocked a hole through the side brick wall and into the kitchen.

Then they produced several lengths of iron pipe and a box of plumbing fittings and screwed and hammered and drilled until, there it was, a shiny brass tap on the wall, just above the big old-fashioned square, brown earthenware sink.

One problem remained even with water on tap.

If you used this marvellous new water provider you had to remember to put the plug in the bottom of the sink because, with no drainage of any kind in the cottage, it didn't go anywhere but the floor underneath.

So the now-redundant water bucket became the "slop bucket" and was left under the sink permanently to catch the waste.

When the bucket was full the contents were thrown out onto the garden—and it seemed to get full pretty often now that the water didn't need carrying from the old well.

Washing oneself wasn't too much of a problem. With water on tap and a gas stove in the kitchen it was just a question of boiling a kettle and getting on with it in the sink.

Bathing, though, was a different matter and required a little more planning.

In the early days the only way of heating any quantity of water, either for the weekly wash on Monday or the weekly bath on Friday, was to light the fire under the old built-in copper boiler in an alcove in the corner of the kitchen.

Every spring the starlings nested in the flue pipe, a fact you discovered as soon as the fire was lit because the fire wouldn't "draw" and filled the room with smoke.

For several days it would then be a battle to keep the pipe clear of nesting materials. As soon as you cleared it the stupid birds would restart their nest-building so that by the time you wanted to use the boiler again the flue was blocked once more.

A concerted effort, however, usually got them to realise that they weren't going to get a nest ready to receive eggs unless they moved. And they generally did move, flying off with many a noisy protest to look for a more hospitable household.

Later came the era of the gas boiler with a flexible pipe which enabled it to be connected to a special point behind the gas stove. It could be lit up, turned off, emptied, disconnected, carried out and stowed away, providing gallons of hot water without the need for newspaper, kindling wood or coal.

Then there was the bath itself.

It was, in common with many other household utensils of the time, made of galvanised iron.

It was long and deep and flat-bottomed. It had a handle at each end and it hung, when not in use, by one of these handles, on a big nail banged into the brickwork just outside the back door.

The bath had to be lifted down, carried over the back door step into the kitchen and lowered onto the floor. It was filled, with the aid of a large saucepan, from the copper or the gas boiler, cold water added to personal taste (not too much because the metal bath itself absorbed a lot of heat) and, if soap, flannel and towel were to hand, you were ready to begin.

Emptying the bath was even more complex.

With the added weight of the water it was quite impossible to lift it outside. So you had to bale it out, saucepanful at a time, until the load had reached manageable proportions when it could then be humped out and upended onto the garden.

In summer it was quite pleasant to take the weekly dip.

In winter the unheated kitchen was about as cosy as a butcher's meat store and I would light both burners on the gas stove to try to cheer the atmosphere a little.

And on those wintry nights we all sat before the big range fireplace in the living room. Heavy curtains were hung across the three doors which led out of the room in an effort to cut down on draughts.

But you still roasted at the front and froze at the back.

By the single gas light above the mantelpiece we would sit and listen to the radio. It was one of those big walnut box-shaped sets that needed an enormous battery to run it and an acid-filled accumulator that had to be carried carefully down the road to the local garage to be recharged about once a week.

In fact we had two accumulators, one on the set and the other at the garage being charged and they were swopped over every Saturday morning.

One of my fondest memories is of my regular Tuesday evening treat, listening to the radio version of Richmal Crompton's "Just William" who, at the time, was my ideal of what every boy should be.

My ideas haven't changed very much either.

While listening I would tuck into my supper, a big bowl of home made thick pea and ham soup, made by boiling a bacon hock, one of the cheapest and most delicious joints available, shredding it into the stock and cooking with cornflour and lots of dried peas that had been soaked overnight.

A doorstep slice of fresh crusty bread to dip into the dish completed the feast.

During the evening a couple of clean wall bricks were put into the oven of the range. When bedtime came they were good and hot all through.

Each was wrapped in several layers of newspaper and placed in a thick cotton bag with a draw-string top, made specially for the purpose from some old cast-off garment.

That was our bed warmer. And a darned good job it made of it too.

Off up the wide, creaky oak staircase we went, candlestick in hand, climbing the outside edge of the wide, ninety-degree curve in the middle because the inside was too steep and narrow.

And if, in the morning, we had chilblains on our toes from falling asleep with our feet on the hot brick, well, there was always the magical "Snofire" ointment to soothe the terrible itching. But life in the cottage wasn't total discomfort.

Within a remarkably short time we had learned that living in the country did have certain attractive compensations for those willing to take advantage of what the countryside had to offer.

Not least of these compensations was the fact that in the nearby river were any number of plump trout just waiting to be caught. As long as it could be done without being caught yourself!.

Fresh trout soon became—and remains—one of my favourite dishes.

3: TICKLED TO DEATH

THE finest trout streams in the world are to be found in Hampshire, from lovely winding little brooks to the truly great angling rivers of the Test and Itchen.

They carry crystal clear water, filtered perfectly by the chalk layers of the rolling Hampshire downland—and they hold an abundance of beautiful fish.

These streams, especially in the upper reaches, are the habitat of the true wild-bred native brown trout, the fish that is most elusive to the fly fisherman.

They don't run to any great size, not compared with the great rainbow brutes now being taken from hatch-stocked, pellet-fed still water reservoirs. Nor do they attract such avid attention from the angling Press.

But for sheer beauty, vitality and, above all, taste, I'd choose a one-pounder from the River Loddon any day. Provided, that is, it's taken well upstream from that river's confluence with the murky Thames.

They're tricky all right.

Even using the very latest in fly fishing rods, precision-built reels and expensive tapered lines, the angler who arms his cast with Iron Blue, Small Black Smut or Blue Winged Olive still has a lot to do before his fish is in the pan.

Many's the time I've watched, fascinated, from the suitable cover of the bankside undergrowth, as a "master" in the art of trout fishing whipped the water almost to a frenzy in a vain effort to connect with a good one.

For my own part I have rarely experienced much difficulty in bringing home a brace of decent trout to the dining table. But then it's all, I suppose, a question of ethics—or technique, depending on how you look at it.

The easiest trout catching I ever enjoyed came during a few glorious weeks one summer when the river authority decided to dredge "our" stretch of the river.

Hour after hour we watched in wonderment as the monstrous dredging machine, with its caterpillar tracks and huge, extending arm, reached out to crash the great grabbing jaws of its bucket "head" into the bed of the stream.

It was easy to imagine some terrifying primeval beast gorging itself beneath the surface of our river.

As it raised its huge head and swung its neck towards the bank, water poured in gallons from between its vicious, ill-fitting jaws and water weed hung, like shreds of the flesh of some unfortunate animal victim, from its teeth.

Each time the bucket arched over another mound of mud, silt, gravel and vegetation was dumped with a gushing flop-of-a-noise onto the growing heap along the side of the river.

And we watched with knowing attention.

From time to time we were rewarded with the sight of a quivering, shimmering shape as a fish, dredged up in the bucket along with the weed, was left stranded and helpless on the pile.

Then there was a race for it. The trout was raked within reach with sticks—the silt and mud was much too soft to venture onto—and several pairs of hands scrabbled to hold it.

Once held, it was knocked on the head with a stone and we returned to our vigil to await another unfortunate victim.

And the big bonus was the encouraging smile of the attractive Land Girl (that dates it!) who amazed us all with the single-handed handling of the fearsome dredger monster.

I'm convinced that for those few weeks we all fell hopelessly in love with her.

But all this was merely a temporary, once-in-a-lifetime method of fishing. Our usual way was with (slightly) more conventional tackle.

While scorning the use of a bread-baited hook (how unsporting), I'm blowed if I could see why one shouldn't use such a perfectly natural bait as a live worm, particularly if one's had the sweat of digging for the little perisher to start with.

In fact I have to confess that when first told by a disapproving adult that trout should be caught "on the fly" I thought that this must be some new infallible bait.

I tried it out for a couple of hours using a hook baited with dead houseflies, swatted with a rolled-up newspaper as they pitched onto the warm surface of our half-open back door which caught the sun nicely.

But it didn't seem to work and I thought at the time: 'Lot YOU know about catching trout, Mister'.

I suppose I started poaching trout at a pretty early age.

I could have been only about nine or ten years old, and certainly didn't consider it a crime, when I marched proudly up the village street on my way home from the river with my first ever, speckly brown trout dangling in full view from the end of my makeshift beanpole rod.

After all, there were plenty of fish in the river, food of every kind was not exactly plentiful, so they were naturally there to be caught.

On that famous day my equipment consisted of a bean pole taken from the garden, a length of button thread "borrowed" from mother's needlework basket, a small cork from the neck of a medicine bottle, a shop-bought number eight hook on a nylon trace and, of course, the worm.

Just below the wheel house of the ancient Lower Mill, that stood less than half a mile from our cottage, the stream rushed through the narrow, brick-lined channel that was the mill race. It was only a dozen feet wide and it was there that I been advised, by an older poacher, to try my luck.

The surface of the water was nearly six feet below the top of the retaining wall where I had to stand and the stream foamed and boiled below in a series of swirls and eddies caused by the force of the water cascading over the mill head.

It was noisy too, as the constant rushing sound of the water blotted out all others, a fact that made me even more aware that I must keep my eyes skinned for trouble in the shape of over-sensitive owners or river keepers.

I dropped my tackle into the race and watched as the cork bobbed furiously about in the current, sometimes racing away downstream, sometimes almost stationary, and once swinging back upstream along the base of the wall where some unseen underwater obstruction had set up a back flow.

Then, quite suddenly, I was almost paralysed with excitement as the cork dived violently out of sight beneath the heaving surface.

I shook myself into action, yanked on the pole and, for the very first magical time, felt the quivering and thumping that is a good fish well and truly hooked.

It is the sensation that no-one who has ever caught a fish of any kind will ever forget.

But hooking a fish and landing it are two very different things.

With no reel and a virtually solid rod there was no finesse about playing it out. In any case the water was far below me and at that time I hadn't even heard of a landing net.

So I just heaved that fish, twisting and jerking, bodily out of the water, up the side of the wall and onto the bank, hoping all the while that the thread line would hold, that the trace wouldn't give way and that the hook wouldn't come adrift.

As luck would have it the landing was accomplished without mishap (although I was to lose more than a few attempting the same manoeuvre at that spot in the future) and there was my first trout, a nice fish of just under a pound, flopping about on the grass.

Back at home, after my triumphal parade through the village, it took no time at all to have that fish cleaned, scaled, grilled in butter and on my plate. I don't believe I have ever enjoyed a meal so much.

That was only the beginning of my "apprenticeship", largely self-taught, in the art of trout poaching.

One young ruffian I knew always boasted that he could "snatch" a trout with a wire on a pole and although I never saw him perform the trick I have known of water keepers who used the same method of taking unwanted pike out of trout fisheries.

The general idea is to creep along the bank until you spot a decent fish "riding" the current within reasonable reach of the edge. Then, while lying as far as possible out of sight, you gently slip the pole into the water, just downstream of the intended quarry.

At the business end of the pole you have a copper wire rabbit snare whipped securely in position so that the noose, with its easy-running metal eye, can be made to stand out firmly from the end.

Your pole is then very slowly and carefully manoeuvered forward towards the fish and the wire noose worked delicately into position about it.

It can be very tricky getting the snare just right without touching the trout as the refraction of light caused by the water makes your pole look from the bank as if it has a sharp kink in the middle.

But eventually it is possible to ease the wire around the fish's middle. A rapid jerk or snatch and you (hopefully) have a nice dinner dangling on the end.

Another method my "snatcher" friend employed (and this one I can vouch for, having assisted him on a number of occasions) was his "tin can" trout catcher.

Thinking back, this individual had come up with some pretty amazing schemes for the illegal taking of game of all kinds and this was one of his best—or worst, depending on how you looked at it.

He had scrounged or pinched a number of empty five-gallon oil drums, then cut out the tops using a hammer and chisel—and a considerable amount of elbow grease—before burning out each one to get rid of the residue of oil or whatever other noxious concoction the drum had held.

Next, he pierced the bottom and sides of each of the drums with dozens of small holes, using the same chisel.

He finished up with what looked like a collection of old-fashioned night watchmen's braziers.

Wading into the river at a stretch where some good fish had been seen, he sank one of the drums into the water, placing it on the gravelly bed of the stream with its open end pointing downstream.

This process was repeated with the other drums until he had four or five traps in position, each placed, as far as possible, behind or beside a patch of growing water weed where they were practically invisible to the casual observer on the bank. He, however, knew the position of each one exactly.

After allowing that part of the river to "settle" for an hour or so he returned to the bank and proceeded to rush up and down the riverside, clapping his hands, shouting, jumping up and down and, for good measure, throwing stones into the water.

The resident trout, not very surprisingly alarmed at these wild antics, streaked for cover in the nearest available weed bed.

Like as not, one would hurtle straight into the "safety" of one of dancing boy's oil drums.

It was the work of only a minute to wade in and heave the drum, fish and all, out of the water and on to the bank.

The holes in the drum allowed the water to rush away but were not big enough to let the fish through. The pressure of the escaping water minimised the possibility of it flipping out over the rim.

The most care was needed when actually lifting the drum. You had to get a strong grip on the rim and hoist the open end up and clear of the water before the poor trout realised what was going on and was able to make his escape.

Worming, snatching, drumming. But none of these methods really holds a candle to the real trout poacher's art—for art it is—of tickling.

To tickle a trout successfully is perhaps the ultimate achievement for a poacher, and one which needs very considerable practice and patience.

Old-fashioned prints or etchings of so-called trout ticklers at work invariably show the participant lying full length on the river bank, shirt sleeve rolled up to the elbow, one hand out of sight below the surface, presumably tickling a trout.

Very picturesque but quite inaccurate. In fact, just about impossible.

I've never seen it done that way and I reckon I've tickled more trout than most.

For a start it's extremely unlikely, to put it mildly, that even the most experienced trout man could stalk a fish to such an extent as to get literally within arm's reach of it from the bank. Ask any fly fisherman.

The slightest movement on the bank, the merest ripple in the water, and any fish worth its salt would be careering off for cover in midstream.

Then I defy anyone—supposing they have managed to overcome the first obstacle—to grab a healthy trout of any sort of size, underwater, with one hand, and get it safely on to the bank.

Take it from me. It can't be done. Not like that anyway.

Inevitably I suppose it was Colley who first showed me how.

Even at his tender age (he was only a couple of years older than me) he seemed to be the only one who knew anything about anything I considered was worth knowing.

Like tickling trout, for instance.

'Come on,' he said, quite out of the blue one day. 'Let's go trout tickling'.

'I don't know how to,' I had to admit.

'Then it's about time you learned'.

Colley was tall for his age, and skinny too, which made him appear even taller. He had pale, carroty hair, very pale blue eyes and a biggish, boney nose which made him look older than his fourteen years.

I'd often thought that the spots of melted butter on the surface of a partly-cooked rice pudding looked very much like the hundreds of pale freckles that covered Colley's face. His arms, too, were blotched with bigger freckles throughout their wiry length.

He never said very much.

Whenever he joined our gang's "expeditions" he very often quietly took charge but he was just as likely to be off doing something on his own.

He was always the one who would know where an owl or a kingfisher was nesting, when and where the frogs were spawning, how to find a slow worm or grass snake, where a doe rabbit had made its nest burrow. And he didn't let many secrets go. So when he offered to teach me trout tickling I jumped at the chance.

Colley not only told me what to do, he showed me how to do it. Several times. He instructed and encouraged. He even kept watch for grown-ups, especially farmers and gamekeepers, while I attempted my very first successful tickle.

After that it was just a matter of practice.

If I practise enough I might one day be as good as Colley!

This is how you tickle a trout.

The first essential is a reliable companion who can keep watch on the bank.

From there he can see into the water more clearly to look for a suitable fish to catch. He can also keep a lookout for such unwanted intruders as the riparian owner, water bailiff, Law, or any other nosey parker.

The tickler, you see, has to get INTO the water.

Whenever I've set out to tickle trout I've chosen a good clear stretch of water that's no more than two or three feet deep with plenty of good weed cover, though preferably not choked with great beds of weed. Lots of smallish clumps are better than one big one.

A pair of shorts or swimming trunks and a short-sleeved shirt or sleeveless tee-shirt are the best gear. Old plimsolls (I suppose I should say old trainers now) are useful to protect the feet from the gravelly river bed.

In you get.

Then you begin to wade upstream, keeping a close watch in front of you. But almost every time it will be your colleague, higher up on the bank and keeping pace with you, who will spot the first likely victim.

Trout like to "ride" the current of the stream, keeping virtually stationary, just moving to one side or the other or rising slightly in the water to investigate every titbit carried down by the flow.

You approach, having been given the location by your partner, moving always upstream. Wading down the current only clouds the water in front of you as your feet disturb the silt and shingle.

'Further up. No. Over to your right. That's right. Beside that weed bed. Ten yards in front of you now'.

The instructions are called from the bank and you follow them carefully until you see the fish yourself.

As you draw near the odds are that it will dash off upstream a few more yards with a series of rapid flicks from its powerful tail. Should it disappear from your view your accomplice will almost certainly be able to put you back on course with a few simple directions.

You continue your slow upstream stalking.

After two or three runs of a few yards at a time the trout will eventually opt to dive for safety into the cover of a patch of weed. Usually it's that bright green stuff with tiny leaves that grows, very thickly, in rounded bunches with a few fronds waving in the current behind it.

And if you're lucky, the bunch won't be too large. Maybe only three or four feet long and a couple of feet wide.

Now the problem is to locate the exact spot in the weed where the fish, invisible at last to both the tickler and the watcher, is lying. And you must find it without causing it sufficient alarm to send it streaking away on another run.

First of all you must get close. Very close.

So you wade up behind the weed bed as silently as possible, taking care not to cause ripples to run forward to your fish's hiding place.

It may take some time to reach the weed without making too much disturbance and you must now get your feet into a comfortable position, just astride the tail-end of the weed bunch.

Once there you slide your hands—both hands I need hardly add—down into the water between your feet and then slowly on forward to the back of the swaying green oval.

To reach it comfortably you will need to bend over almost double with your face nearly touching the surface of the water.

Then, with the fingers moving very gently and very slowly, as though stroking the weed, your hands begin their search.

Carefully and delicately forward they move through the waving strands.

This is usually one of the most (forgive the pun) ticklish parts of the operation.

Every part of the weed has to be systematically searched, the fingers brushing and stroking their way through the clump.

At last, and again with some luck, you make contact, usually with the fish's tail. It's very sensitive so your fingers must ease forward slowly towards the bulge of the body.

It is now your "tickling" really begins.

With the finger tips still moving so very, very gently, you start to caress the trout's flank. Just one finger at first, then, if the fish shows no signs of making off, with two, or three or more. Use both hands, stroking each side of the trout simultaneously. The fingers must move agonisingly slowly and softly. Tickling can't be hurried.

Often the fish will move, altering its position of rest in the weed, then settle again. You just wait until it's still and begin again.

It may take five minutes or more, crouched over a patch of weed, legs and body as still as a waiting heron, with aching back and fingers beginning to go numb in the water and standing up to your thighs in the river.

But you must get the right "feel" of the fish before you ease your hands into position for the final act.

The aim is to manipulate your hands so that the fingers of the right hand are gently and loosely circling your fish just forward of the tail, at the point where the bulge of the body begins. The left hand must take its position circling the body just behind the head.

But you must be careful not to touch the moving gill covers or fins at this crucial stage or your fish has gone like a flash, usually doubling back and fleeing downstream between the arch of your parted legs to disappear in the muddy trail made by your feet.

All the time your fingers must keep up their delicate, caressing motions along the trout's body and belly, exerting no more pressure than that created by the swaying strands of weed among which the fish reposes.

At last your hands are in position.

The fingers, moving still, now begin to form a much closer circle around each end of the fish's body. But still no pressure is applied.

Finally you are ready.

Both hands close, quickly and firmly, to form two tight, vice-like bands at head and tail.

If your luck's really in a few strands of weed get caught up between fish and fingers and these provide valuable additional gripping power to hold the slippery body.

You've still not done yet.

Many a fish in the hand has proved to be too much of a handful to become a fish in the pan.

Make no mistake, a large, live trout, held by wet hands, wants some hanging on to. Soap in the bath has nothing on this.

It is slippery, slimy, and writhes, twists and wriggles in the most disconcerting manner. Not only must your hands and fingers grip tightly around the fish's body, they must also keep up an even pressure towards each other so that the natural shape of the trout assists you to pinion it within your grasp.

Held firmly in this way, the trout is now lifted carefully clear of the water and CARRIED to the bank. Once out of the river take it several yards from the water's edge and dispatch it with a blow on the head with a stone or piece of wood.

Never try to throw your catch onto the bank.

I tried it only once.

Having spent a great deal of time and concentration in getting hold of a nice fish of about a pound and a quarter I thought I'd just heave it out. But it's difficult to get any distance with two hands and I watched in dismay as I saw my intended supper land in the grass at the top of the river bank—only to plop back into the water with a couple of flips of its tail.

Be safe.

Walk out with it.

That way you don't see your fish disappearing halfway to the next parish while you are left, empty handed, to mouth a few choice oaths and contemplate fish fingers instead of tasty, fresh trout.

There was a time when half a dozen of us decided to go into the trout poaching business big-time and we never seemed to be short of customers for our catch at 6d (two and a half pence) for a nice sized fish.

We worked broadly on the lines of the "tickling" technique but by this time had managed to mechanise the art to a certain extent.

Instead of one "spotter" there were lookouts posted on each bank. And instead of a lone "tickler" four or five of us were in the water.

Keeping roughly abreast of each other we moved slowly upstream like a line of beaters on a Bengal tiger hunt.

And to save the long and laborious task of "tickling" we had each armed ourselves with a home-made hand net.

We used thick galvanised wire, like farmers use for fencing (and a farmer's fence was usually our source of raw materials), twisted to form a ring of about eighteen inches diameter, complete with short handle.

To this ring we attached the "net" itself. We made some from old flour bags (these were the days when flour was sold in tiny linen "sacks", not paper bags), some from fine mesh string netting (usually "borrowed" from someone's garden), or, as a last resort, from cast-off stockings previously belonging to mothers or older sisters (most of which I suspect had not actually been cast off in the first place).

As we waded up the stream the bankside watchers would call out their instructions.

'There's a whopper gone into that big patch of weed in front of you, to the left. No, not that bit. Yes, that's the one'.

In the face of this mass invasion the trout would dart and dive for cover. When one did take refuge the nearest "net-man" would be guided to the spot from the bank.

When the exact position was confirmed, the net was lowered into the water and brought carefully up behind the weed. It was then held steady, just behind the weed patch, the mesh billowing softly downstream.

Then, using either the spare hand or a foot, the weed was thoroughly "dragged" from front to back.

At this treatment the hidden fish usually turned and rocketed away downstream—straight into the net waiting only a foot or so behind!

When you felt the thump of the fish in the back of the net (you couldn't see it because of the mud and sediment disturbed by the raking of the weed) you quickly scooped it up and carried it to the bank where the waiting spotter took over.

He clouted the fish over the head, threaded it through the gills onto a piece of string, and handed you back the net so that you could rejoin the hunt.

The netters in the water would pause at this until you were back in line and the search could continue.

One fine summer afternoon we did a few hundred yards of river in this manner and took fourteen trout of a pound and upwards in less than an hour.

The smaller ones we put back "for another day".

How sporting we were!

My personal best was eight in one afternoon during which I had the distinction of capturing two good fish simultaneously in my single net. One of them was the best fish of the day, weighing in at just over two pounds.

We didn't always sell our booty though.

Occasionally we would decide to have a meal at the waterside. Well, it had probably been several hours since we had eaten and nobody was ever in a rush to go home.

We had an ideal method of cooking, prompted, I seem to remember, by a chapter one of us had read in a book on Red Indians—Native Americans we would say now.

After cleaning and washing, the fish were carefully wrapped in large green leaves, dock leaves being ideal.

Then we dug a hole, about a foot square by six or eight inches deep, the bottom of which we lined with more dock leaves. The wrapped fish were placed side by side in the bottom of the hole and more dock leaves piled on top. A few big clean stones were scattered over the top for good measure.

We built and lit a good "camp fire" above the pit, using dry wood from any nearby hedge or copse.

We would then sit around and chat about the day's catch. How Ray had caught that beauty. How Tony (it was always Tony) let a big one get away. We'd keep the fire going hot and strong all the while.

When we got tired of talking, or got too hungry to wait any longer—never more than an hour—we let the fire die down, raked away the embers and dug down into the hot and steamy cooking pit.

It might not sound particularly hygienic but the trout came out of that hole done to a turn, steamed a delicious milky white right through, with just a hint of pink.

And didn't they taste grand!

Outings such as this had to be carefully planned to make sure we weren't interrupted by kill-joy adults (gamekeepers and water bailiffs being the worst).

But, oddly enough, some of our most memorable escapades, like our first contact with strong drink, happened almost by accident.

4: CABBAGES AND THINGS

THEY held a flower show in the village every year on the Recreation Ground (the Rec, we called it).

It wasn't just an ordinary flower show. They called it The Grand Annual Flower Show and Fete. The whole field was taken up for the entire day and tents of every shape and size were erected round a roped-off arena.

In the big marquee was the flower show proper, where scores of trestle tables were loaded with such interestingly labelled exhibits as "gooseberries: culinary" and "chrysanthemums: yellow, curved or incurving".

Fruit and vegetables, home made jams and wines, flowers in profusion, sponge cakes, hens' eggs (brown, of course) and a hundred and one other items combined to fill the tent with a strange, almost sickly atmosphere of inseparable aromas.

In silent, serried ranks the plates, dishes, jars and vases stood, like troops before the inspecting general, awaiting the critical eye of the judges.

And when the judging was complete the competitors and the public were allowed to troop in to see whose entries had won those coveted little coloured cards which denoted first, second, third or highly commended (a polite way of saying that your oak leaf and elder pith wine wasn't really good enough for a prize this year).

And it was then that comments about a rival's "onions, autumn sown", overheard by a third party and relayed back to the criticised gardener, broke up for another year the uneasy truce which had taken the previous twelve months to establish, leaving whole local families refusing to speak to each other until at least Christmas.

Meanwhile, outside, the other activities of the day were getting under way.

Sideshows galore, like bowling for the pig—with the little squealer on view for all to see in a little straw-filled, net covered trailer,—hoopla, coconut shy, guess the weight of the cake (and it helped to know who'd baked it!) how many peas in a bottle, darts, children's sports of all kinds, cycle races, tug-o-war. The list on the programme seemed endless.

And above all the bustle and noise, in fact at times drowning out everything else, came the music over the public address system, interspersed with the occasional high pitched, ear-splitting whistle that seemed to plague the amplification systems at all local shows.

I remember only two or three different tunes blasting out across the showground, few pieces, it seemed, being thought suitable for such occasions. Those few were played over and over again, with breaks every dozen bars or so for the tinny voice of the man at the microphone to announce: "The ladies' three-mile pursuit cycle race is about to start" or "Will the parents of little Jimmy Bond kindly collect him from the secretary's tent".

One of my most vivid and endearing memories concerning the flower show was the blaring, metallic strains of the "Post Horn Gallop" or the "William Tell Overture" echoing down the lane that led to the Rec. You could hear it at least half a mile away.

This annual village show was steeped in antiquity and could be traced back about two hundred years when the main attraction seems to have been the village "knock-out competition".

Whether or not that was its official name I don't know but it is an apt description.

The game, if such it could be called, required all the young men of the parish to gather in the central arena where, at a signal from the judges, they proceeded to lay about each other with cudgels.

The rules were quite simple.

Whoever was left standing at the end won the contest. The prize, appropriately, was a new hat!

Not surprisingly that particular tradition did not survive into the time in which I became interested in the show. Competitions had, thankfully, progressed to a more civilised form.

As youngsters we were able to choose between the painting competition, the collection of wild flowers, or the sack race. These weren't exactly in the same league as the old head-bashing game, especially as spectator sports, but were infinitely more satisfactory from the point of view of the runners-up.

One other unusual contest did, however, fire our young imaginations and enthusiasm for a time. It was the "White Butterfly Wing Collection" competition.

In a well-meaning endeavour to help the horticulturalists of the village (it was, after all, the annual showcase for all the gardeners of the area), the show organisers offered a prize to the child who could collect most wings of the cabbage white butterfly.

What you had to do was catch your butterfly, pull off its wings (not a game for the squeamish, this) and put them in a jar.

On the morning of the show the jars were to be labelled with the name of the collector and the number of wings collected.

The owner of the jar with the most wings received the, then, splendid cash sum of five shillings—25p in nowadays money—at a time when five bob really was worth five bob. This was a very interesting proposition indeed.

'Look,' said Marv. 'It's not much good us all competing against each other. There's not enough butterflies to go round'.

Marv was the brains of the bunch. We all accepted that he was the brightest because he had just passed the eleven-plus exam to go to grammar school.

'What we've got to do is pool all the wings we collect, enter them for the competition under one name—and then share out the prize money'.

It sounded too easy to be true. A simple way of earning a bit of extra pocket money.

So five of us decided to join forces, with the promise of a shilling (5p) each to come when the prize was won.

And so it was that the world's first, and I suspect, only, Cabbage White Butterfly Wing Collection Syndicate was formed.

For weeks before the show we spent every hour we could spare chasing white butterflies all over the countryside. We still didn't seem to be doing too well when Marv had his second great brainwave.

'Look, they want us to catch butterflies to keep them off the cabbages and things, don't they?' he asked.

We nodded in unison.

'Well. Where's the most cabbages?'

'Dunno,' we all chorussed.

'Down the 'lotments of course,' said Marv, with a little more than a hint of exasperation in his voice.

'Down the 'lotments there's hundreds of cabbages and cauliflowers and brussels and stuff. My old man's got some brussels down there for a start,' he continued.

'I bet it's lousy with butterflies'.

And it was.

The village allotment gardens were right next to the Recreation Ground and when we arrived we were greeted by the heartening sight of dozens of dancing, darting specks of white shimmering over the plots.

With a concerted yell of triumph we surged into battle. That first prize was now surely ours!

Swinging our jackets and pullovers as butterfly swots we rushed among the neatly laid out rows of fruit and veg.

But our articles of clothing were cumbersome weapons and seemed to be flattening more brassicas than butterflies.

Then someone, probably Marv, hit on the idea of using a thin, twiggy length of brushwood as a flail to knock the fidgety-flying insects to the ground.

The tops of pea sticks proved to be just about ideal, as well as readily available, and several rows of prize peas were soon wilting from lack of support.

Out on the allotments, with no hedges or fences to get in the way, we found it easy to catch up with our quarry. If we sometimes forgot, in our haste, to run around the neat little grassy paths that divided the individual plots, well, we just ran straight across.

Two friends, homing in on the same target butterfly from opposite directions, failed to notice each other and suffered a nasty clash of heads which resulted in both of them rolling in agony into somebody's strawberry patch.

I roared through a clump of well-grown rhubarb, tripped over a rusty upturned bucket, half hidden among the leaves where the gardener had "forced" a few stems earlier in the year, fell, and ploughed up half a row of young carrots with my nose.

'Got another one,' yelled Marv jubilantly.

'You hit me with your stick, you great clot,' yelled Colley.

'Ouch, my head,' moaned Ripper.

'I thig I'be broag be doze,' I wailed.

'Oh sod. I've knocked another sprout plant over,' exclaimed Mike.

It's fair to say that we made a considerable impact on the number of butterflies attacking the greenstuffs on the allotments.

It's also fair to say that the butterflies we caught probably wouldn't have done half the damage we seemed to manage in catching them.

Finally, some of the plot tenants got wind of what was happening and threatened dire consequences if we didn't vacate the allotments.

To be honest the actual words they used were considerably stronger than that so we vacated in a hurry.

'Miserable, ungrateful sods,' muttered Colley as a parting shot—though not so's any of the irate gardeners could hear him

But our work was done. The day of the show arrived and we had worked wonders indeed.

Our carefully collected wings almost filled one of those old-fashioned two-pound jam jars—you don't see them any more—and although I can't remember exactly what the final tally was it was one hell of a lot. At four wings per butterfly it must have run into thousands.

We put Marv's name on the label, as it was his idea in the first place, took our jar along to the special children's competition tent, handed it in to the lady in charge and sat about impatiently, though confidently, awaiting the call to step up and receive our five shillings first prize.

Imagine our dismay and disbelief when we found we hadn't won!

We came second, it's true, but second prize was only half a crown. And we probably wouldn't even get Marv's name in the local paper.

A tanner each didn't seem much reward for all those hours of toil (especially when we already had a shilling in mind) and anyway it cost 3d to get into the show. That is, if you paid to get in.

To set the record straight, we always took a "hedge ticket", climbing through the hedge into the showground at a remote corner to avoid the man collecting money at the entrance gate.

Nothing daunted, we laid plans early for the following year.

This time we formed an even larger consortium of butterfly hunters and started putting wings into a jam jar as soon as the first unfortunate (and innocent) Brimstones ventured into view, some weeks before the cabbage whites appeared.

This time money didn't count. Our honour was at stake.

So ten of us took to the fields and gardens. Once again the local allotments resounded to the echoing sounds of swishing sticks, clashing heads, whoops of glee, yells of pain and other more general noises of destruction.

And this time we made sure.

Although not such a prolific year for cabbage white butterflies in our neighbourhood, testimony, we believed, to our own efforts the previous summer, we managed to collect even more than before.

We went through the same procedure with our entry and, at the show, waited arrogantly for the results to be announced.

We were second again!

The shame of it!

It seemed to us impossible that someone could have pipped us yet again for the five bob prize and fleeting fame in the show results column of the local Press. But there it was, printed out for all to see on white cards in the competition tent.

'Hang on a bit,' said Marv. 'Look who's won'.

We looked.

On the winning entry was the same name that had appeared the previous year. What's more, we all knew him and we were sure he hadn't got an organisation like ours.

In fact we doubted whether he could actually raise the energy to catch a butterfly. Yet there it was. He'd won the five bob, apparently on his own. No mates, no helpers, no syndicate, no gang.

What we thought was even odder was the fact that he just happened to be the son of the lady who organised all the children's competitions—including the butterfly wing collection.

And it was obviously part of her job to dispose of all the old wings at the end of the show!

Highly suspicious, we investigated further.

The jars were still on display for the public to look at and admire. His two jars were standing right at the front, bulging with white butterfly wings while he stood smirking nearby.

One of the jars looked as though it might have seen better days. Like it could have been used before to exhibit white butterfly wings.

And the other one, well that looked kind of familiar too.

'That's the bloody jar we entered last year!' exclaimed Ripper. 'I'm sure of it'.

'Yeh, and I recognise some of the wings inside,' exclaimed Mike.

With the stark realisation that all was not cosily innocent with the administration of the children's competitions came resignation that we obviously couldn't beat the "system". And there was no way we could join it either.

As a direct result we gave up chasing butterflies and succeeding generations of cabbage whites were allowed to continue their predation on the greens of the local allotments.

We turned our attention to other things.

Ripper, for example, in spite of the fact that he was almost blind in one eye—perhaps even BECAUSE he was almost blind in one eye—became a dab hand both at darts and bowling for the pig. I shouldn't mind betting that he's won more pigs at local shows than anyone else in the country. Probably deserves an entry in the Guinness Book of Records.

As for darts, he went on to become the local star, in later years going right through to the finals of a national competition. He's now a dab hand on the bowling green.

Each year when the show was over the Recreation Ground fell strangely silent. The man who operated the loud speaker equipment had packed up and gone.

The competitors had gone.

The crowds had gone—and so had the contents of the flower show tent.

They, in fact, went in an interesting and rather exciting fashion. Each entry was auctioned off after the show, lot by lot, in a flurry of activity. The idea was to raise a bit of extra cash to help pay the quite enormous administration costs of running the show, tent hire, PA system, lease of tables and chairs and the like.

The auctioneer, a dapper little man in a tweed suit, was a village resident and a partner in a local firm of estate agents and valuers. He was well used to sales, though usually calling prices considerably in excess of those realised by this particular auction.

Each year this individual volunteered for the job and his smiling face and shiny bald head would keep bobbing up and down through the gathering throng of people as he made his way from table to table.

He was agile too, for his age. Probably in his sixties he would, nevertheless, hop up on top of one of the trestles, hold up each lot in turn for the bidding and jump down again—only to reappear as he mounted the next table in line.

And he really got the auction going with a swing.

'How much for this lovely bunch of mixed flowers?

'Won second prize they did.

'Thrupence?

'Do I hear thrupence?

'Come on George, take the missus home this peace offering. You've been in the beer tent all afternoon!

'Home-made plum jam.

'Delicious!

'Must be worth fourpence.

'Do I hear fourpence?

'Be nice on the old man's bread and butter, Mrs Smith!

'The bidding's over here with Harry.

'No more?

'All finished?

'It's yours Harry'

Flowers, vegetable marrows, embroidered cushion covers, all came and went in a frenzy of bidding.

And in the absence of an auctioneer's hammer, obviously of no use to a man standing on a wobbly table, the auctioneer would clap his hands to clinch the sale.

You had to be quick to make your offer. No time to ponder. Hold it high, knock it down, on to the next.

In half an hour the marquee was cleared and all the arguments about who-grew-the-best-what were over for another year. And even as the sale was going on, helpers were piling the trestle legs and tops in one corner ready for collection.

Meanwhile, outside, more show organisers were busy dismantling all the things that they had so painstakingly erected earlier that day.

The thick hemp rope around the arena was untied from its wooden stake supports, coiled and stacked away.

And those same wooden stakes, driven into the ground with many a grunt and groan by two men using a four-handled tubular iron rammer, were now being just as laboriously pulled up.

The trestle tables and folding wooden chairs used by all the officials joined the pile in the big show tent and some of the smaller tents were being taken down.

Then there was the beer tent. There was always a beer tent at the annual flower show and all afternoon its merry trade had been in full swing.

Now, with darkness beginning to fall, the open front had been laced up and the brewery lorries had driven away.

This was the time we enjoyed most about the flower show.

Every year when the show was over we crept back into the empty tents to play.

The beer tent was our favourite and made a first class covered soccer pitch. As long as we didn't make too much noise—which would mean interruption by meddling adults—we could carry on undisturbed until the last of the volunteer helpers had gone home.

Then, our games could become a little more boisterous as, in the deepening dusk, we progressed to wrestling, hide and seek around the many boxes of equipment piled inside, tripping over the guy-ropes outside and, finally, when we were sure no-one else was about, sliding down the tent roofs.

This year we congregated, as usual, in the beer tent, attracted like moths to a candle flame, by the mysterious mixed odours of dew-damp canvas, wet grass and stale beer fumes.

First item on the agenda was a thorough inspection of a huge stack of beer crates filled with brown one-pint beer bottles.

No luck. They were all empty. It was quite obvious what a large proportion of the men of the village had been doing all afternoon!

A search of the boxes and cartons revealed nothing. No lemonade, no fruit juice, not even a tonic or a soda water.

Our investigation having drawn a blank we got on with our game.

It was Colley who spotted it first.

A large beer barrel standing on its own in a corner of the tent.

When I say he spotted it first, that's not quite true. We'd all seen it, of course, but had thought nothing more of it.

It was Colley who had made a closer inspection.

'It's full,' he announced with quiet satisfaction.

‘Full of what?’ someone asked.

‘Full of beer. Wha’d’ya think?’ replied Colley.

This was an entirely new situation.

Every year we searched hopefully for anything the brewery men might have left behind, mouthing many a complaint about their meanness and untrusting attitudes in clearing the tent of its entire liquid contents.

This year it was different. We gathered around. Colley scratched at his mop of uncontrollable straw-coloured hair, pondering a way to get at the treasure trove inside the barrel.

‘There’s a plug down here, near the bottom,’ called a voice, triumphantly from behind the barrel.

We all grabbed hold and heaved the barrel round. Sure enough, there it was, a plug or spigot or whatever they’re called, a little three-quarter-inch thick wedge of hardwood.

Colley tried to pull it out. Only about half an inch stuck out of the side of the barrel and it was stuck fast.

Colley kicked it. No good. After a few moments thought he disappeared outside, crawling under the canvas wall of the tent. A minute or so later he was back, holding half a wall brick in his hand, acquired from heaven knows where.

He gave the plug a tap. First one side, then the other. The plug stayed firm, obviously driven in by an enthusiastic brewery man using a wooden mallet. In any event, it wasn’t likely to fall out again in a hurry.

In a short time we lost interest.

‘You’ll never shift it Colley,’ I said. ‘It’s in too hard’.

Colley didn’t reply. He just kept tapping with his wall brick.

‘Sod that,’ said Ripper. ‘Let’s get on with the game’.

So we did. We all did.

All of us, that is, except Colley. He continued with his tap, tap, tapping with the brick. One up, one down, one on the left side, one on the right side. We left him to get on with it.

The score had reached about 5-4 when there was a sudden scream from the corner.

'HELP!' yelled Colley.

We rushed over.

There he sat, the wooden plug was on the grass beside him and an amber-coloured fluid was streaming out of the hole in the barrel and over his trousers. Then he managed to get his hand over the hole.

'Quick!' he shouted.

'Great. Great,' we all chorused.

'Hurry!!' roared Colley.

'Good old Colley,' we cried enthusiastically, slapping him on the back.

'For Christ's sake. MOVE!!!' he screamed.

Colley sat there, dripping beer into his socks and looking for all the world like the little Dutch boy who held back the sea and saved the village by sticking his finger into the hole in the dyke wall.

'A bottle. Get a bottle,' croaked Colley.

'Where do we find a bottle?' someone bleated feebly.

Colley nodded towards the corner at the far side of the tent.

'There's a bloody great pile of empties over there, ain't there?' he yelled.

Without another word there was a rush for the pile of crates.

Grabbing an empty pint bottle in each hand we raced back to the barrel.

Colley took his hand away.

More beer cascaded over his trousers until the neck of the bottle was juggled into position.

Within a minute we had a kind of production line system in operation with Colley's finger as the tap and someone else holding empty bottles in place, one after the other. The rest of us plied back and forth between the pile of bottle crates and the barrel, bringing more empties for filling.

Yet another stacked the newly-filled bottles out of harm's way.

In a remarkably short time we had what we calculated was probably enough for our immediate needs—about 30 pints of beer.

Colley fumbled the plug back into the hole in the barrel, giving his clothes yet another drenching as he did so, and clouted it home with his wall brick.

We were all anxious to try our "liquid gold".

One or two had already taken secretive little sips and either spat it out or gave exaggerated grimaces of disgust.

But it was up to Colley to try the first "official" swig.

He gulped a couple of good mouthfuls down as we watched in awe.

'Beautiful,' he announced finally, trying to keep the smile on his face.

We all hastened to try it.

'Great'.

'Yeh. Great'.

'Terrific'.

From sheer bravado we all agreed that it was the most wonderful drink we'd ever tasted although, looking back, I'm sure most of us were nearly sick.

'What is it?' I wanted to know.

Nobody knew for sure, except that it was "beer".

The beer that we didn't drink (and that amounted to about 29 and three quarter pints) we decided to store for another day.

The problem was that the bottles, being metal crimp-closing type, couldn't be re-sealed, though at the time that hardly seemed important.

We crept out of the tent, handing the bottles through one at a time under the canvas sides, and carried our hoard to the hedge where there was a favourite hiding place in the bottom of an ancient hollow tree.

We reckoned that we'd got enough beer that, carefully rationed, would last almost until the flower show next year.

Safely stored in the hidey-hole, the bottles would be out of sight until we wanted another swig.

Perhaps tomorrow night.

By now it was pitch dark and long after the time that we would reasonably have been expected to be at home. So, saying our goodnights and promising to meet again the next day, we made our way out of the showground.

We all had the smell of beer on our breath but that didn't present any real problems. We didn't have to breathe on anyone.

But Colley smelt like a brewery.

His trousers, shoes and socks were soaked with beer and what he told his mother when he got home I really can't imagine. Except, knowing Colley, he must have come up with some unbelievably believable explanation.

Next evening we gathered again at the old hollow tree, as arranged, for another drinking session.

It had been a long, hot day and the bottles had no tops on them. We all had a few more swigs. Swigs that put most of us off beer for years to come.

Our beautiful beer was luke warm, very flat, and tasted horrible!

Never mind though. A sizeable chunk of the summer holiday still stretched before us, including the short but hectic rabbiting season.

This was when a fleet-footed boy with a stick could, for a few weeks, become almost a hero, in his mother's eyes at least, through his regular and very welcome contributions to the family food ration.

Catching rabbits was an art that had to be learned at first hand. No text book here.

Advice from adults was sound but sometimes that advice needed a bit more thinking about before being acted upon.

5: RUN RABBIT RUN.

It was late August.

The sun beamed down hotly out of a perfect summer sky and I stood, a diminutive figure in plimsolls, shirt and grey short trousers, in the corner of the big wheat field, waiting to catch my first rabbit.

'If you can get close enough to put salt on his tail,' my grandmother had confided. 'You can catch him!'

I was about five years old at the time and it seemed too easy to be true.

But off I trotted, armed with nothing more than a spoonful of salt in a twist of brown paper, and a lot of faith, to try my luck against the bigger boys at catching rabbits in the harvest field.

Almost straight away I noticed that all the others were carrying sticks. Those arriving at the field without such weapons were soon busily cutting and breaking them out of the nearby woods and hedgerows.

As the afternoon progressed it all seemed a bit unfair to me.

There they all were, charging around the field catching bunnies left, right and sideways while I was still standing in the corner of the field, waiting for one to come within salt-throwing range.

Before very long the harvesting was finished for the day, the last sheaf cut and tied and the last rabbit chased.

And I set off for home, disappointed and empty-handed, my paper-twist of salt intact, to try to explain away my failure.

Grandmother was right about catching rabbits, of course. My only trouble was that I hadn't got close enough.

Mother was sympathetic. 'Never mind. Try a stick next time dear,' she said with a little smile. And suddenly the mystery was solved.

Of course you have to get close enough to a rabbit to drop salt on his tail.

But once there you clobber him across the back of the head with a stick. Simple really. It's just a matter of interpretation of the rules of engagement.

Within a few years I had mastered the rules so well as to be one of the top rabbit catchers in the neighbourhood and every summer holiday found me ranging over a wide area of the countryside, looking for the first signs of the new harvest and the start of yet another short but hectic rabbit-chasing season.

In the normal way a human doesn't have a chance of catching a rabbit in a straightforward running race. They leave you standing every time.

But in the harvest field things were different. The thick, spiky stubble of the new-cut corn, poking up four or five inches tall, slowed the rabbit down considerably while having virtually no effect on the speed of a fleet-footed lad.

Everything got sort of evened out.

Then it became a much fairer test of speed and stamina. Except that, for good measure, the rabbit would start to jink and dodge, sometimes doubling back through your legs at lightning speed, once you began to overhaul him.

In those days of the old reaper and binder machine, and before myxomatosis decimated the rabbit population of Britain, every cornfield had its band of hopeful young rabbiters at harvest time.

The "binder", drawn by a tractor (in earlier days a horse would have done the job) had an odd, bottom-shaped metal seat on the top where the farmhand, often one of the farmer's sons, sat in solitary splendour.

His job was to keep a careful watch to make sure the cutter blades were working, that the windmill-like arms were doing their job of laying the standing corn over against the knives, that the canvas elevator was carrying the cut corn up into the machine, and that the sheaves were coming out the other side, all properly tied up with twine.

Every so often the tractor driver brought this noisy, rattling contraption to a halt as the result of a signal from the binder man banging on the top of the steel-sheeted, red-painted cover of the machine with a long stick carried specially for the purpose.

This contrived clanging was about the only thing the tractor driver could hear above the general din. And anyway he would most of the time be concentrating on looking to the front, keeping the tractor on the right course.

As the odd combination came to a stop both men would dismount for a short discussion on whatever problem had arisen.

Then it was a case of a new reel of binder twine (usually only a few minutes, especially if one of the potential rabbit chasers could be persuaded to run over to the corner of the field, where the spare reels were stacked, for a replacement).

Repairs to a leather holding strap on one of the canvas carriers, or the replacement of a cutter blade, broken off against a large flint, would take a little longer.

Sometimes a few hefty clouts with a large hammer, somewhere underneath, seemed all that was necessary to get the binder back into working order.

And sometimes a major breakdown had occurred which required the summoning of a special engineer from the agricultural equipment merchants in the nearby town.

Several hours could be lost in the wait for him to arrive in his van to put the machinery right.

The harvest continued, smoothly or otherwise, the binder circling the field endlessly, removing just a five-feet width of standing corn at each circuit, and leaving a tidy lane of evenly-cropped stubble, alongside which ran a neat trail of round, twine-tied sheaves.

Gradually the stubble area grew larger and the circuits of the binder smaller as the corn was cut until, at length, perhaps after a full day's work, only a small triangular shaped plot of standing corn remained.

Meanwhile other farm workers had been standing up the cut sheaves into "shocks" of six or eight and these ranks of little tent-shaped constructions were now covering much of the outer part of the field.

This was the time we had been waiting for.

The rabbits which had made their temporary home in the corn crop had been driven gradually into the centre of the field by the clattering of the circling machinery and the hot scent of the sweating harvest workers and waiting rabbit boys.

Now they could retreat no further.

A rabbit's only chance of escape now was to break cover from what remained of the standing corn and race for the safety of the holes of the warrens, or "buries", in the hedgerow.

And we were waiting.

Each time a grey-brown form emerged cautiously from the corn a shout went up. At first it would lope quite slowly away from the noise of the harvester, then, when it realised humans on foot were closing in, it would gather speed towards the hedge, until it was running flat out.

'There's one! Heading towards the woods! Hey! Quick! Cut the bugger off!'

A boy, maybe two or three boys, even half a dozen, gave chase.

As often as not, the fleeing rabbit would find a gap in the defences and make a successful home run to the hedge well in front of a string of shouting hunters.

'Hi-yi-yi-yi-yi! Hi-yi-yi!'

I don't know why but it seems to have been traditional to yell at the top of your voice while chasing a rabbit. The theory, I imagine, was that it terrified the rabbit into immobility. In practice, I found it simply got me out of breath more quickly.

Those rabbits that managed to reach the safety of the hedge were usually followed by a hail of last-effort, wildly-thrown sticks and a string of abuse.

Those that didn't were quickly clubbed, grabbed up by the closest runner and dispatched with a rabbit punch behind the head or a slick wrist-flick which broke the neck.

When harvesting in the field was finished all the rabbits that had been killed were laid out in a couple of neat rows beside the now strangely silent binder, parked near the hedge close to the gate.

The farmer and another worker ignored them as they, with apparent casualness, continued with the job of winding down the binder's road wheels, fitting the towbar and generally making it ready to be dragged out, sideways, down the lane to the next field waiting for harvest.

A crowd of eager young faces clustered round the catch.

The bag was counted. Then counted again. Everyone in turn, it seemed, had to count them. More talk. Half-whispered arguments about who had killed what and how many.

'I got three. That's one of mine'.

'No you didn't. Anyway, that one's mine'.

'Here he comes now'.

'No. They've still got to crank up the drive wheel'.

'This is the best catch this year'.

'We caught more yesterday over at Newnham'.

Finally the farmer, his work on the machinery preparation complete, approached the circling group.

He pushed his way silently through the throng of expectant watchers and waiters.

Then he, too, stooped and counted, deliberately and carefully, ignoring the offered advice of all the youngsters who already knew the score and were now pressing around, sticks resting on the ground, hands resting on stick tops and chins resting on hands.

‘Thirty-two,’ he announced finally and a dozen small heads nodded their agreement. A fair day’s catch but by no means a record.

He crouched on his haunches to inspect the corpses more closely, picking them over, feeling one here, feeling one there.

Half a dozen of the youngest and best he laid aside for himself and his workers.

Then, for the first time, he looked up and took a good long look around the circle of eager, waiting faces.

‘Here, you’.

He tossed a rabbit to one of the bigger boys whom he recognised as one of the ones who had been in the harvest field most of the day, a fact that always went down well with the farmer as it helped stop rabbits sneaking away, out of the field, at quiet periods during the day, like when the binder broke down.

He picked up another and handed it to me.

‘You better ‘ave one. I seen you catch a few’.

Round the faces his searching eyes travelled. He was going to give away no more than he considered absolutely necessary. Some boys got a rabbit. Some didn’t.

‘You didn’t get ‘ere ‘til after we finished. Sling yer ’ook’.

‘One fer you. You ’elped with the shockin’.

‘What’s your name? Didn’t I jest give one to yer brother?’

On one occasion I was presented with a rabbit for no better reason than that, by asking my name, the farmer discovered I was the son of a girl with whom he used to attend the village infants school thirty years earlier.

Perhaps six or eight would be distributed.

Then it was: ‘That’s it then’.

And whoever hadn't got one by now knew they weren't going to get one. Not today at any rate.

The score or so of rabbits left would soon be hanging in the window of the local butcher's shop. And the farmer would have a little more ale money in his pocket.

Those of us lucky enough to receive rabbits made our way back excitedly to where we had left our bikes in the hedge beside the lane, chattering and laughing as we went.

The others, disconsolate, kicked at stones and clods of earth on their way out of the field.

Later, pedalling home, they would talk loud and long about "that mean old sod" but for the moment they were tight-lipped and silent.

We all had our favourite rabbiting sticks and it was something of a minor disaster if you lost or broke it.

When going for a new stick I always looked for a good thick clump of hazel, well inside the wood, where the stems grew straightest, up towards the light.

I wanted one that was not too thick, no more than three quarters of an inch in diameter at the top, widening to an inch or so at the bottom. Any thicker and it became too cumbersome, both to carry and to swing while running at full speed.

And I searched until I found such a hazel stem growing from just above ground level on the "crown" of the hazel clump. Instead of cutting it I would lever it out and down until it tore away from the main stem, leaving a broad, slightly bent, club-like knot on its lower end.

It was then trimmed to length—just about waist high—and the handle end polished up smooth with my hanky.

This was the stick I would hope to carry right through the harvest season, perhaps next season too. It would go with me on my bike, tied with two pieces of string along the underside of the crossbar and, by September it would, with luck, have twenty or more rings cut neatly in the bark below the handle, one for each rabbit killed.

A great deal of discussion took place about sticks. Some rabbiters carried long ones, some short, some liked thick ones, some thin. I always favoured one on the light side as I found that a smack from an inch-thick hazel was as effective in stopping a rabbit as a swipe from a miniature telegraph pole.

There was one boy who carried a stick that was really no more than a wand, springy, and no weight at all. Yet he always seemed to catch his share of rabbits.

One day, having arrived late and breathless at a harvest field without a stick (a dreadful admission) I decided to experiment by doing without.

I had already made the necessary inquiry: 'Are they running yet?' And had been told; 'Just'.

So there was really no time to cut a stick anyway.

I was already a faster runner than most and I reckoned that not carrying a stick would give me an extra yard or two on my rabbiting rivals.

Then, I theorised, I would have time to tip my rabbit over with one foot and pounce on him.

In all fairness it has to be said that the theory was absolutely correct.

Five of us set off after one rabbit and after fifty yards I was well up on the rest of the field.. By the time the rabbit started to tire, at which point he began to squeal, I was five yards to the good.

My foot went out, tipping the exhausted rabbit neatly onto his side and in a flash I was on him.

As I dived the other pursuers arrived, line abreast. And as my hands closed over the furry grey back four heartily swung sticks whistled through the air to crash in unison onto the back of my head.

I saw a large number of dancing, silvery lights against a dark background and immediately lost all interest in the rabbit, which was hastily snaffled by one of my so-called friends. I rolled over, blood pouring from a nasty cut in my scalp. Other lumps started to rise and throb under my hair.

Two of the others sat me up and they all started dabbing at my wound with an assortment of hankies, most of which had obviously already had a number of other, just as dubious uses.

'Wha'ja get in the way for?' one indignant hunter wanted to know.

I didn't answer.

Shakily I got to my feet. The two most concerned of my colleagues helped me as I stumbled to the hedge. Then they left me, sitting in the shade, while they finished their hunting.

Later they took me home, supporting my weight between them and struggling to carry both me and the rabbits with which each of them had been rewarded.

My head was injured and so was my pride. I was also empty-handed. And that was the first and last time I ever tried rabbiting without a stick.

Sometimes a chance discovery in a harvest field would dispense with the need to test the lungs to bursting point in a mad chase.

Occasionally the passing binder would reveal what at first glance appeared to be a small, elongated mound of loose soil in the stubble. We knew that it was a rabbit hole.

Not the kind of hole you find in the bank or the hedgerow, connected underground by yards and yards of tunnel to perhaps a dozen others. This one would invariably be a temporary and probably disused breeding burrow.

The pregnant doe would leave the communal bury and find herself a patch of soft earth, very often in a growing crop of clover or corn, where she would scrape a shallow tunnel. It would be only three or four feet long and at the end of it, in a slightly widened chamber, she would build her nest of hay and pieces of fur pulled from her own body and give birth to her litter of young.

In a remarkably few short weeks the pink-skinned, blind babies would be fed, weaned and would be grown into young rabbits big enough to fend for themselves. They would leave the nursery and return with the mother to the main bury.

This abandoned nest hole was just the place a terrified rabbit would choose as a last attempt to escape the smell and the noise of the approaching harvesters.

And often, if the nest hole was near the middle of the field, more than one of them would get the same idea.

'Look, a hole!' came the cry.

We ran over to make sure it wasn't so old that it had caved in.

No. The little mound of soil was still neatly scraped back away from the dark opening that disappeared at a shallow angle beneath the corn stubble.

Next came the inevitable claims.

'Bags I first!' shouts the one who first spotted the hole.

'Bags second!'

'Bags third!'

The rest call out their claims in turn.

Usually the length of the tunnel is just too great for an arm so one of the rabbiting sticks is poked into the hole.

If it comes to a sudden, solid stop our luck is out but now and again the stick is brought to a halt by something firm but with a little give. The stick is withdrawn and the end closely inspected by several pairs of young but experienced eyes.

A few fresh hairs adhering to the end of the stick confirms that there's a rabbit down there.

Before an attempt is made to reach it we check the area around which we estimate the end of the tunnel to be, to make sure no emergency "pop-hole" has been added to the burrow. We've all seen quite enough supposed certain dinners cheat the dining table this way.

If there is a bolt-hole, someone places a foot over it and we're ready to start

The burrow is never more than a few inches deep and the roof can be torn up easily by eager hands. Soon boy number one is lying on his stomach, one arm out of sight down the hole, his upturned face a study of concentration.

His searching hand eases its way along the tunnel until it touches the rabbit. All he can feel is the hard rounded rump as the frightened creature tenses and tries to get a fraction of an inch further away from the groping fingers.

One finger works its way under the rabbit's rear and is crooked round one hind leg at the "ankle", a job made easier by the length of the rabbit's back foot.

With a grip on just one leg—the fingers have still to find the other—it's well nigh impossible to drag a full grown rabbit out of a narrow burrow.

'Got 'im?'

'Yeh. No. Sod it. Not yet. Yeh, that's it'.

Eventually both back legs, or at least the feet, are gripped and the rabbit is drawn firmly out, the jubilant hunter getting first to his knees and then to his feet.

The rabbit is held upside-down by the back legs. He holds his head back with his ears laid flat against the spine, front legs bunched forward and clawing at empty air.

A smart chop with the side of the hand at the back of the neck and he's dead. His head hangs down, ears go floppy and, after a few spasmodic jerks he is still.

If there's another in the burrow, boy number two may have to dig away a few more handfuls of tunnel roof to reach him. Then that rabbit gets the same treatment as the first.

I've seen as many as five rabbits crammed nose to tail in such a tiny burrow. It certainly made the easiest rabbiting I ever knew.

There were certain unwritten laws attached to rabbiting in the harvest field. If you wanted a rabbit they had to be strictly observed.

Bigger boys enhanced their chances of being rewarded at the end of the day if they spent an hour or two helping the farm workers standing up the shocks—called "stooks" in some parts of the country.

If the binder ran out of twine, one of the boys would be expected to run over and fetch a replacement spool from the sack by the gate.

You never got in anybody's way, especially not a farmer or guest with a gun. In any case some of those armed with shotguns were best avoided totally, like staying on the far side of the field.

And on no account, even in hot pursuit, would you dare to chase a rabbit into the standing corn.

If it did double back into the crop, and they often did, you just had to wait for it to come out again. And if it decided to reappear on the opposite side to where you were waiting, then you had to run around the corn before you could begin the chase again.

Odds were, of course, that either it would make the safety of the hedge before you could get on terms again or someone else would be guarding that side and "your" rabbit would be accounted for by a rival.

Rustling movements in the corn could be very deceptive.

I once saw a contemporary slash down with his stick at a sudden swaying motion in the edge of the corn which had caught his eye, then pick up a magnificent cock pheasant with a broken neck!

He might have got away with it except that the local gamekeeper happened by pure chance to have arrived at the field to see how things were going only a few minutes earlier.

The boy was escorted off the property by the keeper with many a dire warning about what would happen if he saw him in another harvest field that summer. And, of course, he didn't get to keep the pheasant.

On another occasion, a rabbit which had crouched low as the cutters went overhead, was suddenly pounced at by three of us who were killing time by following the binder round. The rabbit was nimble and leapt straight forward—straight on to the flat base of the moving binder.

For a few seconds it stayed on the canvas conveyor, which carried the cut stalks of corn into the machine for tying, running against the direction of the belt, like a man trying to go up the down escalator, and getting nowhere.

Then it was laid senseless by a single blow from a rabbiting stick.

We watched, open-mouthed, as our rabbit travelled in blissful unconscious splendour along the canvas carrier until it disappeared up into the machine.

Racing to the other side we watched and waited as the big metal rake-like arm swung over to project another neatly-tied sheaf clear of the binder.

We had to search through three sheaves before we found the rabbit, still blissfully unconscious but otherwise unscathed, tied up inside.

We visited a lot of farms, killed a lot of rabbits and usually the farmer operated a pretty fair share-out system.

Occasionally we came across a farmer, more often a younger man, who didn't seem all that interested in rabbits—except that we were helping him to get rid of his pests—and he allowed each of us to keep whatever we managed to kill.

On the other hand there was the infamous day when about fifteen of us accounted for nearly sixty rabbits in old Marksey's big oat field and he didn't give a single one away. Needless to say none of us ever bothered to kill rabbits in any of his fields again.

And I once had the dubious pleasure of being told to "push off" by the farmer as soon as I set foot inside the field.

At the end of the harvesting day it was off home for us rabbiters. The lucky ones, and the cleverer ones, had the spoils of their victories hanging from the handlebars of their bikes, the rabbit's back foot threaded through the hamstring of the opposite leg for ease of carrying.

And it was the hero's welcome home. A rabbit for Sunday dinner meant money saved on a joint and in any case made a delicious change from our usual knuckle end leg of lamb (then a relatively cheap buy).

Once delivered to the kitchen door the rabbit lost its interest for me until came the time to eat it.

Mother, however, had the job of preparing it for table which she did with great skill and precision.

The rabbit was paunched and then skinned. The skin was pulled off whole (after the feet had been cut off) over the skull, taking the ears with it and leaving the head looking strangely bald and staring-eyed.

Next the eyes were expertly gouged out with a sharp-pointed kitchen knife and our rabbit was ready for the oven.

It was roasted whole and served up with roast potatoes, runner beans from the garden, peas and gravy.

We all had our own favourite piece. Dad liked a back leg where there was plenty of good white meat. Mum enjoyed a piece of back or "saddle" because, she said, it was nice and tender. My sister invariably had one of the front legs

Me?

I got the prize for bringing the rabbit home. I got the head.

There wasn't much meat on it—but what a variety!

First I'd pull off the lower jaws and eat the tender little pieces off the side of the jaw bones. Next came the tongue. Small, it's true, but absolutely delicious. Then came the main treat.

With a blow or two from the handle end of my knife I cracked open the skull. Then I could dip my teaspoon into the brain. Marvellous. Royalty could not have wished for better.

As our experience in rabbiting grew we looked for other ways, apart from chasing them around the countryside, to bring one home to the table and to extend the all-too-short season of the harvest.

Some schemes worked. Others, as you will see, were less successful. In fact most were dismal failures.

6: POLECAT IN MY POCKET

THE harvest was over. The season had been, as usual, enjoyable but all too short, crammed as it was into a few short weeks of late summer.

So we turned our attention and our energies to alternative methods of catching rabbits.

As yet, no-one had come up with a system which gave us the same kind of excitement, not to mention the success, of the harvest field chase, though we did try out quite a few.

An old countryman once told me that rabbits have a natural hatred of water (it's probably true, I don't recall ever having seen one swimming) and could be driven out of their burrow by flooding them with water.

Trouble was, none of the buries we ever found was anywhere near within range of a tap or hosepipe, even supposing we had a hosepipe.

Warrens near the river were tried without success. We had only a few odd tin cans and bottles to carry the water in and by the time each small dribble was delivered to the hole, even with a "bucket and chain" system in operation, the previous delivery had simply soaked away into the summer-parched soil a few inches from the entrance.

Another method we investigated looked for a while as though it might be a winner and gave us the chance to try a scientific approach.

Someone, probably Marv, said he had heard you could smoke rabbits out so we experimented by building a fire over a rabbit hole, waiting until it was well alight, then covering it over with dead grass, rotten wood and damp grass.

It certainly gave off clouds of thick smoke but even so, most of it seemed to be escaping into the air. The density of the fumes that did find their way underground was obviously not sufficient to smoke out a chiselbob, much less a rabbit.

Then Marv had another idea—and this is where the science came in.

Instead of using "ordinary" smoke we should use something stronger, he said.

We looked at him blankly.

'Sulphur,' he announced knowledgeably and, I thought, a little over-grandly.

'Sulphur smokes like 'ell. Stinks an' all. That'll fetch 'em out'.

He had obviously begun chemistry lessons at his new school.

It might sound strange today but at that time—not really so many years ago—when chemists made up many of their own presciptions instead of dishing out factory-made pills, one could buy all manner of ingredients at the chemist's shop, simply by going in and asking for it.

Sulphur was not only easily come by, it was cheap as well, only a few pence for a pound, weighed up and sold "loose" in a stiff brown paper bag.

So the sulphur was bought, no questions asked, by one of our number on a special visit to the nearby town.

On the outside of the bag was a white label bearing the name of the chemist and the words "Flowers of Sulphur".

Inside, of course, was the magical chemical that was to revolutionise the country's rabbiting techniques.

To me it looked just like a bag of bright yellow custard powder.

It was late afternoon when four of us set off to try out our new discovery.

In a bank which ran along the edge of a wood, well out of sight of prying eyes, we found an ideal bury. Six holes.

We planned the operation carefully. This time there would be no chance of failure.

One of the holes was widened a little by scraping the soil away from the entrance. Then all the other holes were blocked with pieces of turf, dug up with the heels of our shoes, with large stones or lumps of wood.

Next we got a little fire going in the first hole using nice dry sticks. When it was burning well, with plenty of white hot embers forming, Marv tipped the entire contents of the sulphur bag onto the flames.

At first it seemed to smother the fire completely. Then it began to smoke.

Only this time it really DID smoke.

The sulphur seemed to be burning quite slowly, smouldering really, with just a hint of tiny, almost invisible, blue flame. But it gave off great clouds of yellowish-white pungent fumes that made our eyes run and the breath choke in our throats.

Marv was right about that.

The remains of the fire with the burning sulphur were pushed as far into the rabbit hole as we could get it with a stick. The hole was then blocked up.

We stood back and surveyed the scene.

All the holes were now blocked and tiny wisps of acrid smoke were beginning to work upwards from several different spots where stones or lumps of wood failed to make gas-tight joints at the burrow entrances.

'That's about enough,' declared Marv who had, of course, become our unofficial technical adviser.

'Open up a couple'.

It was done cautiously, two of us doing the unblocking while the other two stood poised, rabbiting sticks held high, waiting to clobber anything which ventured forth.

Nothing.

We waited.

Still nothing.

The fumes were beginning to disperse now. The fire must have gone out. We opened up the rest of the holes.

Of rabbits there was not a sign.

We scraped the dead embers out of the “fire hole”. There was still quite a lot of unburnt sulphur left among the ashes but it was obvious we were wasting our time with this bury. Mr and Mrs Rabbit were not at home.

Anyway, it was getting late so we decided to give the rabbits best. For the time being at any rate.

On the way back across the field on our way home we discussed our latest disappointing and unexpected failure. At the far hedge we paused, standing in the rapidly gathering gloom, to continue the inquest.

Suddenly Marv let out a yell.

‘Christ. Look!’

He was standing, eyes agog, outstretched arm pointing towards the wood that we had left not ten minutes before.

As one we turned and looked.

Orange flames were dancing merrily over the bank we had recently vacated, flickering in among the dry grass and crackling up into the bracken and brambles.

Now and then tongues of flame leapt upwards into the lower branches of one of the trees and a mixture of wood smoke and more ominous yellowy vapour was drifting away into the darkening sky.

‘Come ON!’

Marv was the first to move, legging it back across the field towards the quickening flames. We burst into motion, caught him up and ran, line abreast, towards the ever-brightening fire.

‘You and your bloody sulphur!’ I managed to gasp as I ran.

We reached the wood not a moment too soon and set about trying to extinguish the flames.

The fire was already among the bushes and undergrowth and was spreading rapidly in all directions.

Using our jackets and broken off branches we beat at the flames, stamping and thrashing about like maniacs in our desperate efforts to get the fire under control.

A few more minutes and the whole wood would have been alight and totally beyond our capabilities.

It seemed an age before all signs of flames had disappeared and we made a methodical inspection of every single quarter of the disaster area, checking to make sure that not a single spark was left.

We dug up earth with the toes of our shoes to pile onto suspicious spots and when we came to the rabbit hole where the burning sulphur had been we made double sure.

'Pee on it,' said Marv.

So we did. Then we covered it with earth for good measure.

Finally we felt it was safe enough to embark once more on our homeward journey which we did, tired, blackened, scorched and smelling strongly like an old bonfire.

And rabbitless.

It was about this time that I decided to abandon the scientific approach to rabbiting and I set about finding myself a good ferret.

Throughout the winter I cadged and pleaded to be allowed to accompany the son of a local farmer on his ferreting days.

I did everything I was told to do, watched everything carefully, noted all the intricacies involved in choosing a bury, setting the nets, handling the ferret and retrieving the rabbits.

There came a time when I reckoned I knew everything there was to know about ferreting, although I was to find out that my education had only just begun.

The following year I bought my very first ferret.

It cost me five shillings of hard-saved pocket money, handed over to the farm worker who, I had come to hear, had some young polecat ferrets for sale.

For some reason, never quite understood, I always preferred the polecat to the normal albino ferret.

The albino is almost pure white all over, saving just a hint of sandy yellow along the belly, with watery, reddish-pink eyes. Altogether an evil looking animal.

The polecat, on the other hand, although identical in every other respect, has brown or black markings around the face, on the ear tips, feet and tail and to a greater or lesser extent along the back and flanks. And the polecat has warm brown eyes.

The two types interbreed freely and the resultant pups turn out either "polecat" or "white", may be several of each in the same litter, in much the same way as some dog breeds, like Labradors and Springer Spaniels, can produce a mixture of distinct colour types.

I knew what I wanted. A polecat bitch. The dog ferret, as well as being nearly twice the size of the female and therefore more of a problem to carry, had, I was assured, a bit of a reputation for being a little on the lazy side.

I have since seen plenty of dog ferrets working their asses off with no sign of sloth but at that critical stage I wasn't prepared to take the chance.

And yes, I know the male and female ferret should properly be called a "hob" and a "jill" but dog and bitch is what we always called them.

So after inspecting and sexing the ferret man's entire litter I made my choice and carried my new "baby" home in a cardboard box lined with straw.

Once at home I installed my little "Suki", as I had already named her, in a smart new hutch, custom built for her out of wood and wire with a nice private little sleeping compartment at one end. She settled down quickly and was soon tucking into a helping of warm bread-and-milk sop.

Anyone who tells you that ferrets are nasty, vicious creatures are talking through their hat.

True, if you keep a young ferret in bad conditions, feed it poorly, handle it only on the days you want it to work—and then after starving it for several days beforehand—grabbing at it roughly, using a thick pair of gloves, the odds are that it will turn out to be nervous, edgy and inclined to sink its teeth into you at the first opportunity.

So would just about any other animal.

Properly fed and cared for and, most importantly, handled every day from a young age, a ferret will almost certainly grow up to be a lovable and amusing pet—and no less effective when hunting rabbits.

No need to starve them for a week. Just no food on the morning you work them to sharpen up their enthusiasm. They will hunt as much by instinct and pleasure as by necessity.

And so it was with Suki.

She was hardly more than a few inches long when she came to me. At six months she was all but full grown and would be ready to work the coming winter season.

Ferrets are rarely used in summer because of the likelihood of there being immature rabbits (kittens) in the bury which might be more easily caught and killed underground by your ferret, in which case you have a long wait or a hard dig ahead of you.

A ferret that kills underground is likely to take the chance of a meal, then fall asleep beside the partly-eaten victim.

By early winter the rabbit's breeding season has (at last) ended and the possibility of the ferret encountering a youngster in the bury is remote.

Suki was a typical polecat. Her overall body fur was creamy, shading to almost black along her sides and back. Her little rounded ears were black, as were her face, feet and the tip of her tail. Her markings were not unlike those of a seal point Siamese cat.

From the time she was a baby I took her out of her hutch each day. At that age her teeth, though sharp as needles, had no strength and although she would attempt to gnaw at my hand at first it was, after only a few days, more in play than in earnest and did no harm.

I stroked her, tickled her under the chin and spoke softly to her, as one would a kitten. By the time she was half grown I was letting her run loose in the garden and playing with her, using a little woollen ball on the end of a thread, which she would chase, once more like a kitten.

She would jump, dance and leap into the air with back arched almost double and all four feet off the ground, chattering excitedly all the while.

And I could pick her up, behind the shoulders, any time without the slightest protest from her or fear of harm to me.

When I couldn't get meat scraps from the table I often fed her raw dog meat from the butcher or any small bird I could knock off with my airgun, even bread and milk which she never lost her taste for.

Her bowl was kept clean and full of water and her hutch cleaned out and fresh straw or hay put in every week.

She was the perfect pet. Well, except that, like all ferrets, she had a strong and distinctive odour.

Soon the time came for her to be put to work. I had an old ragged overcoat which I wore for ferreting and as long as I let it hang loose, which it invariably did because there were no buttons, Suki would travel with me happily, curled up in one of the deep pockets. I carried the purse nets in the other.

It was Ripper, who himself owned a polecat bitch called Jo-Jo, who first invited me to go poaching with him.

Our first expedition started pretty disastrously.

Having found a likely looking bury of only five holes in the hedge bottom of a nearby farmer's pasture, we set the nets and put Jo-Jo to work.

Half an hour later she had failed to reappear and Ripper had to run all the way home to fetch a spade.

There followed about another hour's digging before we discovered her. She had a rabbit "hung up" in a dead-end tunnel, couldn't shift him and refused to leave him, he keeping her at bay with vigorous kicks from powerful back legs.

To cap it all, the rabbit eventually leapt out of the digging and made his escape unscathed.

After this little incident we settled down to some serious and often very productive ferreting, coming home with up to a dozen rabbits between us which we sold for one-and-sixpence each (that's seven and a half pence today) to eager neighbours.

We soon learned which buries were occupied and which were unused, or recently ferreted out, by inspecting the entrance holes and looking for signs of fresh digging or new rabbit droppings.

Holes clogged up with fallen leaves we ignored completely.

We always tried to choose a bury with not too many holes.

More than ten or a dozen meant the ferret would have a long job to find and "bolt" the occupants from the maze of underground passages—and that could mean a very long wait.

So having selected our bury of six or seven holes, all of which were reasonably accessible, we set the nets.

Purse nets are made of light but strong string or nylon netting with about a two-inch mesh, fixed at each end to a small brass ring and threaded along each side to a pair of long cords which act like the draw strings of an old-fashioned leather purse, hence the name.

By pulling the two brass rings apart the net sags from the cords like a miniature hammock which can then be opened up to form a circular net about two feet in diameter.

A net was spread over each of the holes, making sure that the cords at the edge were evenly spread around the tunnel opening. A wooden peg, attached to one end of the twin cords, was then pushed into the ground beside the hole with a boot heel.

When all the holes were netted, including the half-hidden pop-holes which could easily be missed under a tuffet of long grass, the ferret was put in.

One side of a net was carefully lifted and Suki or Jo-Jo was eased, nose first, into the hole. Usually, especially if there were fresh signs of rabbit activity, they needed no urging. With an odd rippling walk, that was almost a trot, the ferret disappeared from sight below ground.

We stood back.

Each of us had already agreed which holes we would watch and we stood in silence, waiting for the action to begin.

Sometimes it was five minutes. Sometimes it was fifteen, by which time we would be passing urgent messages to each other by sign language or barely audible whispers. Part of the secret of ferreting is that it must be done quietly, with absolutely no movement once the ferret is in.

As the minutes went by the tension mounted.

Sometimes there came the faintest thumping from somewhere below our feet, the vibration felt rather than heard. An old buck was using a back foot to rap out an alarm to the other occupants and a warning to the intruder, whose scent by now was spreading through the burrows.

Ripper and I glanced at each other and exchanged knowing nods.

Then Ripper gave a tiny whistle.

I glanced up from the four holes I was trying to watch simultaneously to see him nodding towards one of his holes and pointing down without moving arm, hand or finger.

A rabbit was just visible at the burrow entrance, its twitching nose almost touching the meshes of the net which it must have mistaken for a few strands of grass.

It was waiting, watching, trying to decide whether to bolt for it or risk turning back and coming face to face with the ferret underground.

It was the ferret, coming up the tunnel behind the indecisive rabbit, that settled the issue.

The rabbit came out of the hole like a shot from a gun. In a fraction of a second he was in the net, the draw string, anchored by the peg, closed behind him and he was tumbling over and over in a jumble of fur and netting.

The ferret, only inches behind him, half emerged from the hole, blinked two or three times in the light, looked around, decided the rabbit had gone, and disappeared back down below to look for another.

Meanwhile Ripper was on the netted rabbit in a flash.

He grabbed it up, pulling the peg out of the ground as he did so, extricated the rabbit by the back legs, at the same time shoving his foot over the now unprotected hole to stop a premature escape by another.

He quickly and expertly stretched the rabbit's neck, killing it instantly, tossed it, still kicking in its death throes onto the ground, and proceeded to unravel the net.

Once untangled, usually accomplished by a few sharp tugs on the two metal rings, the net was reset over the hole and the anchor peg replaced. Had it been too tangled he would have taken a fresh net from his pocket, leaving the other to be sorted out at a more opportune moment.

Then we settled back to wait once more. With the old buck bolted the ferret made quick work of chasing out the remaining two rabbits in the bury and they were quickly netted, despatched and laid out with the first.

Before long the ferret, tired of chasing around the now-empty tunnels, came cautiously up, had a look around, then trotted out into the open to be retrieved. The nets were collected and folded and we moved on to the next bury.

Ripper carried his ferret inside his shirt, next to his bare skin. He claimed they kept each other warm when there was a nip in the air and Jo-Jo certainly seemed very content with the arrangement.

Suki, I discovered, was not only friendly and docile, she was keen as mustard when it came to hunting rabbits. She would shift the most stubborn buck out of a burrow and once, when Jo-Jo got hung up in a big bury, we put her down as reinforcements.

Within seconds there were rabbits coming out of that warren in all directions and we had the most hectic five minutes ferreting of all time. Eight rabbits caught, three of them struggling in different nets at the same time, and two more escaping from holes we hadn't time to reach and cover.

But don't get carried away with the idea that ferreting is just a matter of pop in a ferret and pick up the rabbits.

At times it can be a long, cold wait with nothing to show at the end. At other times it can be a long, hot slog digging out a hung-up ferret

And sometimes…

Well it happened like this. A boy I knew at school had recently acquired a ferret and kept pestering me, as an acknowledged "authority", to find him somewhere to poach and finally I agreed.

After school one afternoon we set off on our bikes for a place I had in mind several miles away. No sense fouling your own nest, I reasoned.

The cycle journey completed, we left our bikes in the hedge beside the main road along which we had travelled and continued on foot across a couple of fields to a section of the disused and dried-up canal, the banks of which I knew to be the site of some good buries amid the undergrowth of brambles and nettles.

We started ferreting but without tremendous success. By the time the light began to fade we had managed to catch only two rabbits and, worse still, the ferret had failed to show up after some twenty minutes in the last bury.

We stayed on and tried every trick we knew to get the ferret to come out, like making thumping noises with our hands against the ground near a hole and by trying to imitate the squealing of a rabbit in distress, even by shaking on of the dead rabbits in the hole's entrance.

But all to no avail, our ferret remained below.

The ferret had almost certainly killed underground and was not likely to reappear for hours, after it had enjoyed a good feed and a sleep. And, of course, we had no spade. Finally we had to give up.

My companion said he would come back at first light, before he went to school, and try to retrieve his ferret.

Meanwhile we packed the nets and the rabbits we had managed to catch into the sack that the ferret had travelled in and headed for home.

When we reached the main road I thought at first that we must have missed our way in the twilight as I couldn't see our bikes. A quick search up and down the verge confirmed our very worst fears—the bikes had gone.

My bike was nearly new, bought out of pocket money and odd job savings over several years so it was with a heavy heart that I led the homeward trek on foot.

It was pitch dark by the time we reached the cottage and many hours had passed since we left school, without leaving word of our intentions, to go ferreting.

My mother hadn't bothered too much at first about my non-appearance but as tea time came and went and supper time approached with no sign of me she began to worry. After all, I often went missing on various jaunts around the countryside, but rarely missed two meals in a row, especially at night.

As we approached the cottage I recognised her voice. She was by the gate and she was in serious conversation with someone else. It was a man. I soon recognised his voice, too. It was Pc Crank, the village policeman.

It seems she had gone up the road to the police house for advice when I had failed to appear. He had told her go home and wait until he put on his tunic and helmet, then he'd come down to the cottage to take down some particulars about my mysterious disappearance.

Suddenly, at the sound of our footsteps in the lane, the policeman's flashlight clicked on and the powerful beam cut through the darkness, lighting up our faces and momentarily blinding us.

'THERE he is'.

My mother's voice clearly showed her relief at my safe return. Her tone, however, quickly changed to outrage at the trouble I had caused.

'Where have you BEEN?' she demanded.

There was silence from both of us.

'Where's your BIKE?' she wanted to know.

Silence again.

'What've you got in the sack, son?' It was the sterner, deeper voice of Pc Crank asking the questions now.

'Rabbits,' I replied weakly.

'And our bikes have been pinched'.

'And I've lost my ferret,' complained my colleague.

'Good thing too, I should think,' was all the sympathy he got from the bobby.

Of course he wanted to know all about the ferreting lark, where we had been and suchlike. We assured him we had stayed on the roadside verge, public property and all that, doing no harm to anyone, we emphasised.

Pc Crank let it go at that.

Then we all went inside where he took down all the particulars of our stolen bikes in his little notebook, commenting as he tucked it back into his tunic breast pocket that he didn't hold out much hope for their recovery, which, he added darkly, would teach us to look after things in the future, instead of going poaching around the countryside.

He clearly hadn't believed our "public property" line but was obviously not going to take the matter any further.

But luck was with us.

A couple of days later Pc Crank called round to say that our bikes were awaiting collection at the main police station in town. I swear he could have told us sooner had he wanted.

It seems that while we were busily engaged in ferreting an over-zealous AA patrolman had reported that two bikes had been abandoned beside the main road and had been there "nearly all day" which seemed strange as we hadn't left school until four o'clock in the afternoon.

Anyway, the police had sent out a van to collect these abandoned machines and were now holding them in protective custody.

'Lucky for you,' said Pc Crank.

I wanted to say that I'd rather they'd kept their noses out and left my bike where it was, saving us all a lot of trouble. But I remained silent, At least we were getting our bikes back.

Next day my friend and I arrived early at the police station. After formal identification and some form-filling our bikes were wheeled out of the little locked compound.

'Tell me,' said the young constable who performed the handing-over ceremony. 'What were you doing all the time your bikes were lying in the hedge?'

Friend and I looked at each other. I turned to the policeman wearing my most "butter-wouldn't-melt-in-his-mouth" expression.

'Blackberrying?' I offered hopefully.

It seemed not to register with him that winter was almost upon us and that the blackberry season was long past.

But ferreting also had its funny side.

Like the time two farm workers I knew went out for a few hours sport one frosty Sunday afternoon.

Each took his favourite ferret, carried in little custom built wooden boxes with a sliding door at one end and a leather strap for carrying.

In a couple of hours they had accounted for four rabbits between them and were thinking of packing it in, the late afternoon growing decidedly chillier. In fact they were heading back along the hedgerow towards the farm cottages when Harry spotted a likely looking bury of only seven or eight holes in the bank at the foot of the hedge.

'Just do this one quickly?' Harry asked, his breath making little fog-like clouds in the cold air as he spoke.

'Right-oh,' agreed George. 'Then we'll call it a day'.

He put down his ferret box and the sack containing the nets.

Four of the holes were on the near side of the hedge but it was obvious there were two or three more on the far side that couldn't be reached.

Harry took a handful of nets out of the sack, stuffed them in his jacket pocket and, carrying his ferret box, walked a few yards along the hedge until he reached a spot where he could force his way through the thorns and climb the wire fence into the next field.

Then he came back to a position opposite George who was now clearing the holes and setting the nets on his side.

Harry placed his ferret box carefully on the grass and proceeded to deal with the holes on his side in the same way.

A few minutes later the two men were finished. They could barely see each other through the barrier of hawthorn between them and their half-whispered conversation was conducted through the hedge.

'All netted?' whispered Harry.

'Right. All netted,' returned George.

'Ready then?'

'Yep. Ready'.

'Ferret in?'

'Right. Ferret in'.

The two stood back to watch and wait. Not a whisper broke the silence. Not a shuffle nor a fidget interrupted the silence of that cold afternoon.

After fifteen minutes there was still no sign of a rabbit.

'See anything?' whispered Harry.

'Nope. Not a thing,' replied George.

Another ten minutes passed.

'Heard anything?' asked Harry.

'Not a sound,' was George's reply.

When a full half hour had gone by without a sign of rabbit or ferret it was obvious that all was not well.

Each man got down in turn and, on hands and knees, head cocked, ear in rabbit hole, listened for the faintest of scrapes or the tiniest of thumps from underground.

But there was utter silence, made deeper, it seemed, by the cold.

Finally Harry spoke out.

'Well, I'm sorry George, I gotta go. I'm on milkin' s'afnoon. Don't like to leave you hung up like this but I daren't wait any longer'.

And he stamped his feet and flailed his arms against his sides to try to get some circulation back into his icy hands and feet.

George understood and was sympathetic.

'That's all right,' he replied. 'I'll stay on 'ere for a bit. Soon's thet ferret shows I'll bring 'er round to the cottage and put 'er in yer 'utch'.

Harry was puzzled.

'Why d'you want to put 'er in MY 'utch?' he asked.

It was George's turn to be puzzled.

'Well, it's YOUR ferret ennit?'

There was a long pause.

‘I didn’t put my ferret in,’ said Harry. ‘I thought you put your’n in’.

‘No,’ returned George. ‘I didn’t put MINE in. I thought you put YOUR’N in!’

Meanwhile the two ferrets slept blissfully on, each curled up cosily in its little straw lined box…

But rabbits weren’t the only free food to be had for the taking in the country.

In the days before laws were introduced to protect most of our wild birds, nearly all the youngsters I knew were avid birds’ eggs collectors and some collections grew, over time, to quite impressive proportions. My own nearly filled a cotton wool lined drawer of the big old chest of drawers in my bedroom.

Not all the eggs for which we searched so diligently were destined for the collector’s tray.

As the drawer filled up the chances of finding a species I didn’t already have diminished and the hunt for particular specimens grew harder.

So I turned my attention from eggs in particular to eggs in general.

7: RAIDING THE ROOKERY.

'EGGS', as my mother had more than once been heard to remark, 'is eggs. So it don't matter what's laid them'.

A sentiment with which I was in complete agreement.

It was only natural, therefore, that as a result of my wanderings around the countryside, the odd partridge egg found its way into the pudding mixture or the pigeon egg into the pie crust.

I sometimes wonder now if that was the reason why my mother's pastry more often than not turned out like a wet book.

Rooks' eggs, like young rooks, make fine eating but although they build their nests in easy-to-find, big and noisy colonies, rooks do have this unfortunate habit of building them at a great distance from the ground.

Our nearest rookery was in a mixed wood of lime, ash and oak. And practically all the nests were sited in the taller limes.

However, it was on an otherwise blank bird nesting day that we decided the time had come to raid the rookery.

There was just no way that I, with my vertigo, was going to be persuaded to go aloft and I was beginning to think our expedition was doomed to failure before it had begun when Marv, our best climber, announced he was willing to have a go.

We had to give him a bunk-up to get him started onto the lowest branches which were well out of normal reach from the ground but after that he made steady progress up a large lime tree in which we could see three or four separate nests.

He paused for breath, perched nearly a hundred feet above us and swaying gently to and fro as the breeze stirred the smaller topmost branches of the great tree.

Then he clambered on up, up among the ever-thinning boughs, while the disturbed birds kept up a ceaseless, noisy chorus of protesting "caw-caws" as they wheeled and circled in a black cloud above his head.

A few more feet and he peered over the rim of a nest.

'Eggs!' he shouted, his voice from that height coming down to us strangely faint.

We were ready.

We had already worked out a rather ingenious method of collecting the eggs.

Marv obviously couldn't climb down with them, there was too much risk of breakage.

So we had arranged for him to drop them down, one at a time, for us to catch at the foot of the tree in our own version of a firemen's safety blanket—you know the sort of thing, where a ring of firemen hold a circular sheet for people, trapped in burning buildings, to jump into.

In this case the "safety blanket" was to be my jacket. I took out of the pockets all the hard things that were likely to break an egg, like my penknife and catapult. Then two of us held it out between us and we were ready to receive the first egg.

Marv was just about visible up through the branches, appearing, disappearing and reappearing among the early spring foliage as he swayed first one way and then the other in the gentle breeze.

'Right?' he yelled.

'Right,' we chorused.

He let one go and the first of our eggs was on its way.

It appeared as no more than a black speck initially as it hurtled down towards us.

About half way down it glanced against a swaying bough, shattered into a thousand pieces and showered our upturned faces with a mixture of shell, yolk and white.

A goodly selection of oaths and obscenities was uttered as we wiped the goo from our eyes.

'Hang on!' we yelled.

We obviously had to re-assess the situation and after a few moments deliberation shouted up new instructions to the now impatient Marv.

'Wait 'til the wind dies before you drop the next one,' I shouted. 'And try to find a clear space to drop it through'.

It was a bit like asking a bomb aimer to drop his bomb down the chimney of an enemy factory from a height of 30,000 feet.

'Ready?'

'Ready!'

The second egg was released and came sailing down towards us.

Marv did a little better this time.

The egg was only twenty feet above us before it, too, came to grief against a branch. Only this time we were a better prepared and managed to duck and scatter to avoid most of the messy deluge.

'Try it again—but be more careful!'

Marv waited for the swaying to ease, held the egg at arm's length, squinted down through the branches to get the aim right and let go.

This time he was bang on target!

At around this time in my life my new Physics master was trying to instil into my unreceptive brain the fact, among others just as uninteresting, that, because of gravity, a falling object accelerates at a rate of 32 feet per second per second.

I never really grasped what the "per second per second" bit meant.

I now discovered at first hand that what it briefly indicates is that an egg dropped from a height of about a hundred feet is going damned fast by the time it reaches the ground.

In practical terms the result was that the rook's egg, falling into my outstretched jacket, reacted in exactly the same way as if it had fallen onto a slab of concrete.

'Hang on!'

We tried scraping the splattered mess from the material but without much success. Then we held a hurried conference.

'Perhaps,' said Mike, 'we should sort of ease the jacket down just as the egg lands. Sort of cushion the fall a bit.

It sounded like good sense. A bit of "give" in the safety blanket might act as a shock absorber.

'OK! Try again!'

'Right?'

'Right!'

A few seconds later a fourth egg bomb came screaming down.

But try as we might we couldn't get the timing right for "dipping" and another egg spread itself thickly over the back of my jacket.

Marv had now to move on higher to another nest, having exhausted the contents of the first. Our luck was in.

'Eggs!'

Three more times we tried to get it right.

One broke against a branch on the way down and gave us all another egg shower, the other two added to what was now a conglomerate mass on the back of my jacket.

'Hang on Marv! We can't catch 'em!'

We waited in subdued silence as he came back down the tree. My time was spent trying to remove the mess of well-beaten egg from my jacket with a handful of grass.

I was also desperately trying to think of some rational explanation for getting it in such a state. My mother would certainly want to know!

Marv dropped the last few feet to the ground and with a triumphant flourish took a rook's egg, intact, from his mouth. As usual the tried and trusted method had proved to be the only sure way of bringing an egg safely down a tree.

It was then that Tony had one of his rare brainwaves.

'If we had a handkerchief we could lower the eggs down on the end of a long bit of string,' he said. 'If we had a long bit of string,' he added.

It seemed the perfect solution and we all looked at Marv expectantly.

'Stuff that,' he muttered. 'I'm not going up there again'.

But fried, scrambled or boiled, my favourite egg will always be that of the moorhen. Only slightly smaller than a bantam's, with a cream coloured shell generously speckled and blotched with purple and brown, the yolk as bright and golden as a summer buttercup. The "moggy's" egg is delicious.

My sister could never bring herself to agree and whenever she saw me eating them the conversation went to a fairly set pattern.

'Eeurgh! How can you eat THAT?' she would want to know. 'You don't know where it's come from or what's been crawling all over it!'

Little did she suspect that she'd eaten quite a few herself at one time or another, without knowing it, in mum's pastries and pies.

'That's right,' I would reply gleefully, never one to be put off my food by anything, as I took the top off another one and propped it into the top of an egg cup that had been partially stuffed with paper to accommodate my moorhen miniature.

And I would smile again at the disgusted look on her face as I dipped my specially narrow-cut toast “soldier” into the egg and transported another tasty morsel mouthwards.

‘Lovely!’ I assured her.

‘Huh!’ she would retort. ‘You’ll be eatin’ bloomin’ blackbirds’ eggs next!’

She was stupid like that. Everyone knows a blackbird usually lays only four eggs and the size they are you'd need at least a dozen for breakfast.

Not like the good old moorhen.

She’d lay eight or ten and if you found a nest with only one egg in it you could take it, knowing the bird probably wouldn’t desert as most other birds would. She’d just go on laying and you could come back to the same nest and collect an egg every day for a week or more.

One big problem with moorhens, though, they invariably built their nests, using twigs and rushes, well out of reach of the bank of the river or pond.

Sometimes it would be just in the far edge of the reeds, sometimes in a bush or low overhanging tree, often it would be constructed on an odd piece of log or driftwood that had somehow become anchored in midstream.

After sustaining a number of wet feet—and there’s not much more uncomfortable than a wellington boot full of water—I at last devised a method of taking moorhens’ eggs without leaving terra firma.

I pinched a beanpole from the garden and a dessert spoon from the drawer of the kitchen table, lashed the spoon to the end of the pole with a piece of string and I was ready to go, using my new patent keep-your-feet-dry moorhens’ egg collecting apparatus.

Using my new invention I found I could cover a mile or more of river bank in an hour and return home with fifteen or twenty moorhens’ eggs for the larder—and dry feet.

One adjustment I soon found necessary was the size of the spoon on my egg-pole.

At full stretch it wasn't difficult to manoeuvre the spoon into the nest and get an egg to roll into it. But bringing it safely ashore often presented problems.

The weight of the pole, combined with the leverage and the "whip" in its eight-feet length, produced a wobble which, if it got out of control, resulted in the egg being shaken out of the bowl of the spoon and into the water. Sunk for good.

Experimenting with a teaspoon instead of a dessert spoon I discovered that a moorhen's egg fitted snugly into it and although it was a little trickier to get the egg to roll into the spoon in the first place, there were not so many wobbles—and fewer lost eggs.

With more than one person involved in the egg-collecting operation (and we rarely went out alone) we had a simple yet strict set of rules for making sure everyone got a fair share.

'Bags I first moggy's egg!' came the shouted claim, usually from whoever had brought the pole., "moggy" being our name for moorhen.

'Bags I second!'

'Bags third!'

It was like a game of snap. The quicker you shouted, the higher up the list you came.

Tony, who was pretty slow in most respects, was usually last, in fifth or sixth place.

Then it was : 'Bags I first duck's egg!'

'Bags second…'

The same ritual was repeated perhaps half a dozen times to cover the eventuality of finding a wide range of edible eggs from pigeons to plovers.

As we usually stayed pretty close to the river the chances of finding the nests of some species "bagged" was remote. Still, you could never tell. It was just as well to get your oar in, even if it was only for the first claim on a great crested grebe's nest.

Another difficulty which presented itself as soon as you found a nest was how to tell if the eggs in it were fit to eat or whether they contained blood-streaked yolks—or, worse still, half formed chicks.

Coming home with a pocketful of eggs of which half had to be thrown away was almost as bad as coming home with no eggs at all and a wellie full of water.

Several "infallible" methods had been suggested and tried from time to time but each had been found to be wanting to some extent in infallibility, like dropping the egg into water.

If it sank it was all right, if it floated it was "addled"—the term we always used to describe an egg that was uneatable through incubation rather than just bad.

The trouble is you can't really tell just HOW eatable or otherwise an egg is by any method we then knew.

Our answer to the problem was relatively simple.

In the case of a moorhen's nest, or any other bird that produced a fairly large clutch, like pheasant, wild duck or partridge, if there were, say, six eggs or less in the nest we reckoned it safe to assume that the laying was unfinished and that the eggs would be unincubated—and therefore eatable.

Seven or more and we cracked one on the spot on the pretty safe gamble that if incubation had begun, all the eggs would be at the same stage. One OK, all OK and vice-versa. The slightest sign of blood in the yolk and we left the rest of the clutch intact.

The greatest decisions had to be taken if you were lucky enough to find a plover's nest with a full clutch of four, highly prized, eggs. To break or not to break, that was the question.

Or, even worse, a wood pigeon's nest with its full complement of two! If the one you broke turned out to be all right there was no way you could then take it home—and you had lost half your prize!

Many times I faced the dreadful choice.

‘Go on. Break one!’ comes the expert advice of one friend.

‘No. Risk it!’ says another voice of wisdom.

I carefully consider the problem and decide to play it safe. Cracking the pure white shell on the nearest stone I gingerly open it up. A perfect yellow yolk, without a trace of embryo, slurps into the grass.

‘Sod’s Law!’ comes the verdict.

Sod’s Law is the one that states that where there exists a choice between two courses of action and where no other helpful information exists to assist the decision, you will always choose the wrong one!

In its simplest form it operates when you accidentally drop your toast on the floor and find that it always falls butter-side-down.

Nature herself sometimes intervenes in a decidedly odd way on behalf of her less fortunate members.

Having spotted the twig-platform nest of a pigeon high in a particularly formidable hawthorn tree we had to decide who was to go up and investigate. The bird was seen to fly out of the tree so the odds on the nest containing eggs were good.

Our decision was unanimous.

‘It’s Tony’s turn’.

‘No it’s not. I…’.

But argument was useless. It was a foregone conclusion, even to Tony, that he was going to get the thorniest tree, the thickest bramble bush or the muddiest bog.

He began what was going to be a long and painful climb.

The hawthorn trunk, a gnarled and twisted pillar, went up without a branch for eight feet, then exploded into a mass of knotted thorns.

The nest was well away from the trunk, out among the thinner thorny branches. And Tony was pretty bulky. They couldn't possibly hold his weight. We all knew before he started that reaching the nest was a virtual impossibility. It was a task none of the rest of us would have attempted lightly.

But he stuck to it.

'Ouch!'

A thorn went through his sock.

'Aargh!'

He'd grabbed hold of another sharp one.

About fifteen minutes and a lot more yells of pain later Tony was perched high in the thorn tree, still below the nest but now only a few feet away.

'Go on Tone! You're doing great!'

We were all truly impressed by his pluck and tenacity.

Another five minutes of delicate shifting, accompanied by more cries of pain, and he was in a position to peer into the nest.

'Eggs!' he cried jubilantly.

At least his climb had not been wasted.

'How many?' we wanted to know.

'Three'.

There was a stunned and disbelieving silence.

One of the first things you find out about pigeons, wild or tame, is that they only lay two eggs to a single brood. Ever.

'Don't be daft. There can't be'.

'There is'.

'Stupid sod. Can't even count'.

'There's three I tell you'.

'Show us'.

But try as he might, Tony could get no closer and the nest, and eggs, remained out of his reach—and out of our sight.

'Can't reach. But there's definitely THREE eggs!'

'Balls!!'

'Come up and see for yourself then!'

And that's precisely what we did.

After Tony had clambered back down we took it in turns to make that awful climb to get a glimpse of the impossible, three eggs in a pigeon's nest. Because there were!

Even then, none of us was able to reach them and there they had to remain. We all got thoroughly spiked in the process.

Like I said. Nature sometimes has an uncanny knack of getting her own back.

I believe it was Colley who led Ripper and me into a not unrelated phase of our activities when, one day in May, he showed us a kestrel's egg.

We admired the beautiful rounded contour of the thing, its creamy coloured shell, heavily speckled all over with brown. And, of course, we wanted one—or two—for our own collections.

'There were four in the nest and I only took one,' Colley confided.

'Go on Colley, Where's the nest? Tell us where you found it.'

To our surprise he did!

He described the location, down to the very tree, a tall willow standing among other smaller trees and bushes on the edge of the moor a couple of miles away. We recognised the spot from his description immediately as a place we had seen many times when we were out beating with Stan the gamekeeper.

Off we set on our bikes, crossed the last field on foot and arrived at the site Colley had detailed. Throughout the last half mile of our trek we had been beset by doubts about the nest's existence.

Why had Colley been so willing to share his secret?

Would there really be a kestrel's nest there?

Was he even now still laughing at the way we had so willing scurried off on a wild goose chase?

But no. As we approached and the willow tree came into view it was obvious that there was a nest of some sort in its uppermost branches.

As we drew near a bird was seen to fly away.

A kestrel, one of the country's smallest hawks. Colley had been telling the truth!

Ripper started to climb the tree. It had to be him, I was totally hopeless at tree climbing. It was not a difficult climb for him and as he neared the bundle-of-sticks nest we heard an odd, high-pitched screeching sound.

Peering over the rim of the nest Ripper let out cry.

'Young 'uns!'

It had obviously been several weeks since Colley had raided the nest and the remaining three eggs had hatched!

We held a hurried discussion as to what to do, Ripper 50 feet up the tree, me at the bottom. We decided that if we couldn't have a kestrel's egg in our collections we'd have pet kestrels!

So we took all three young hawks home and installed them in an empty rabbit hutch at the bottom of our garden. They were barely past the fluffy stage and were covered in short, stubby young feathers, only recognised as hunting birds by their hooked beaks.

We fed them on food scraps every few hours but, despite all our efforts, the one which was decidedly smaller and weaker than the other two, died after a few days.

However, we still had a hawk each and with cat food, supplemented by raw dog meat from the pet shop in the nearby town, the two birds gained rapidly in size and in a few weeks became fully fledged.

We had taken them out of the cage on many occasions to feed them so they were quite used to human company, happy being handled and were not a bit shy.

At last, with each of them tied on our wrists with lengths of string, we took them up to the Rec to teach them to fly.

At first they just fluttered to the ground but after a while began to stay in the air for ten yards or more—always tethered by the string on one leg. A few more visits to the playing field and we had them flying 30 or 40 yards back to our hands.

Our vague plan was to keep them as pets and go hunting with them—like kings and noblemen of old—although what we expected them to catch I'm not sure, seeing as their natural prey would only have been small voles and large insects.

However our project came to an end soon after.

While on one of her shopping trips to the pet shop for raw dog meat, my mother had mentioned that it was for her son's pet kestrels. At this the shopkeeper had pricked up his ears and said he would like to see them.

An appointment was duly made for him to visit the cottage and we had visions of him offering large sums of money for the birds. The man was late and Ripper, who had to leave before he arrived, said he wasn't going to accept less than five shillings for his.

When the pet shop owner finally did turn up that's exactly what he offered.

'Five bob each son. Wha'ja say?' And he waved a ten-shilling note enticingly in front of my face.

To my shame, and later regret, I sold those two kestrels for a paltry half a quid (50p today) and I don't believe Ripper's ever forgiven me for letting them go so cheaply.

What did the shopman do with them?

Well, we were later told that he'd made a very handsome profit indeed by selling them on to an airfield where they were used to keep other birds away from the runways, thus avoiding potentially fatal "bird strikes". How true that was we shall never know but I would have thought it highly unlikely that a little hawk like a kestrel would have kept anything bigger than a sparrow at bay!

One unforgettable afternoon Colley decided to try for the eggs in the swan's nest that appeared every year on a tiny, reed-covered island in the middle of the river where the stream widened to form a sort of small, slow moving lake.

He started off by taking off his shoes and socks and attempting to paddle across, perched astride a big dead log that was lying at the water's edge.

Not only was the timber so water-logged that it more or less sank as soon as he sat on it, it was also very unstable and he only just saved himself from a complete ducking by jumping clear as the log rolled over.

'Bugger,' he murmured quietly as he tried to wring the water out of the seat of his pants.

Colley spent the next two hours building a makeshift raft with some tree branches and four empty oil drums that he pinched from a lean-to shed behind the village garage.

Tied together with wire and string, the peculiar craft was launched.

Using another branch as a punting pole he set off once more.

This time he fared rather better and managed to stay dry for almost a whole minute—just about the time it took for water to seep into the "watertight" seals of rag he had used to plug the necks of the drums.

As he headed towards the island the "castaway" raft sank very slowly out of sight beneath his feet and it was only by turning and punting furiously that he managed to regain the bank as the water lapped around his knees.

He leapt ashore, leaving his doomed craft to drift away downstream, almost totally submerged, with only the intermittent rippling of a surfacing branch allowing us to trace its progress.

'Bugger!' muttered Colley, a little more audibly as he rung the water out of his socks.

All this time we stayed clear. It was Colley's solo effort and he was determined to do it alone. We were happy to just watch him try.

We thought he might have given up after this latest setback but he just said: 'Wait 'til tomorrow,' and sauntered off home.

Next day he was back as promised and there was an even bigger gallery of spectators lining the bank.

Word had spread around the young population of the village—'Colley's going for the swans' eggs!'

This time Colley had acquired, heaven knows how, the jettisoned wing-tip fuel tank of an aircraft from which had been chiselled a square hole from the metal, just big enough for one small person to squeeze into.

He embarked yet again.

But the ungainly vessel, a sort of a cross between a tiny Eskimo kayak and a fat torpedo, proved to be just about as steady as his original log had been.

We were treated to a unique and magnificent display of arm flailing as he tried frantically to keep the thing upright and he made it back to dry land, having travelled no more than a few yards, exhausted by the effort.

Colley's last great attack very nearly paid off.

He spent several more hours in a work of modification, the ingenuity of which left us wide-eyed with amazement and admiration.

Using two poles, a short length of thick log and several long pieces of string, Colley fitted his boat with a do-it-yourself outrigger.

He climbed aboard and pushed off.

For a paddle he had a home-made affair fashioned from a length of tile batten to which he had nailed a small square of plywood as a blade.

By now the river bank was lined with dozens of young spectators in something like festive mood as word of the attempt spread further afield and a rousing cheer went up from the assembled onlookers as Colley got under way once again.

The outrigger was a huge success.

As long as Colley leaned to the left, the side the outrigger was fixed, the craft appeared to be tolerably stable, although steering it seemed a bit haphazard.

But he persevered and the unlikely looking combination edged away from the bank, crossed the intervening stream, and began to make its perilous final approach to the island.

The swans' nest was a big, untidy heap of vegetation, sticks and rushes.

The pen, which throughout the two-day invasion preparations had remained completely unconcerned, was cradled comfortably on its summit, her long, graceful neck curved over her back, bill buried under one wing.

She appeared to be asleep.

Our cockleshell hero struggled and splashed his way towards her.

He was within a few yards when the female swan stirred, looked up, and seeing the approaching invader, let out a long, angry hiss.

Almost immediately a huge white and menacing apparition, in the shape of the cob, glided into view round the top end of the little island, behind which he had been awaiting developments since the raiding party first appeared at the riverside.

The huge male swan arched his great neck, half-opened his enormous wings—making him look at least twice his actual size—and, with a hiss of anger moved swiftly to take up his battle station between the nest and Colley's boat which had come to an abrupt halt and was now drifting slowly back into midstream.

Its skipper was obviously uncertain and was assessing this new and unexpected development.

Colley was clearly in two minds about whether to call the swan's bluff or retreat.

It was the swan itself that settled the issue.

It spread its wings once more, hissed again and half-swam, half-flew to attack.

All thoughts of swans' eggs were dismissed from Colley's mind as he back-paddled violently.

As the big cob closed for battle Colley panicked completely.

'AOWGH!!' he screamed as he began swinging the paddle wildly, trying desperately to keep the angry bird at bay and his flimsy craft afloat.

A resounding cheer, whether for Colley or for the swan is unclear, went up from the watchers ashore.

The ferocious swan made a kind of passing run which gave Colley an opportunity to get his paddle into the water again.

By this time the boat had drifted some way downstream and the paddler's efforts finally managed to get it back towards the safety of the bank.

The swan, meanwhile, stood off, watching carefully.

But the invasion was over.

Colley got back ashore, shaking.

‘Sod that for a game of soldiers,’ was his only comment.

And that was the first and last time that any of us tried to take a swan’s egg. What a relief to get back to the moorhens.

Almost as memorable as the swan incident, though not nearly so enjoyable as a spectator sport, was the situation which developed from another of our regular egg-hunting expeditions, an episode which left us not only a little sadder but also a little wiser.

8: THE EGG AND US.

FIVE of us set out that early summer day with high hopes of a good bag of wild birds' eggs.

The sun beat down out of a cloudless sky, hardly a breath of air stirred and the heat haze shimmered over the surface of the road and across the standing corn in the fields beyond the hedge.

It was one of those days when, hatless, you could put your hand on the top of your head and feel your hair almost too hot to touch beneath your palm.

We left the dust of the tarmac road and struck off across country to try our luck along the hedgerows, headlands and woods in our search for the nests of pigeon, partridge and pheasant before going down to the river, our favourite hunting ground.

All the while we carried with us our trusty moorhen nesting pole with spoon attached. In any event, some of the woods we were to pass on the way had hidden little ponds, secret overgrown pools of near-stagnant water, which moorhens were known to have used in previous nesting seasons.

But although the day could not have been more perfect our luck was right out and two hours of diligent quest found us as empty-handed as when we had set off from the village green, our habitual meeting place.

That was the situation when, at mid-morning, we decided to abandon the woodlands and hedges and go all-out for moorhens down by the river.

At that point we were still a mile or so from our destination and our route lay over several fields, picking up the line of a local public footpath, and on through Mr Marks's farmyard down to the river.

In spite of the fact that we were on a public right of way we approached the farm with caution and not a little apprehension.

Old Marksy, and he was not unique in this, had more than a few times found it necessary to chase us off his hayricks, out of his young cornfields and, on the last occasion, away from his calf pen.

Hayricks, you see, make ideal things to slide down, especially when you pull a few armfuls of hay out first and set them down beside the rick to land on.

The farmer's main complaint seemed to be that large areas of the protective straw thatching covering the rick used somehow to get loosened by our boots and go sliding to the ground with us.

Nowadays, of course, hay is formed into tightly packed square bales and stored in covered barns. Alas, modern youth is thus deprived of yet another enjoyable rural activity. I'm naturally referring to the hay that is not turned into haylage or stored as silage.

Cornfields, particularly when the young corn is still green, make exciting places for games and battles of every kind.

By crawling along on all fours you can make intricate little paths and passages in secret patterns over a wide area of the standing crop, another pet hate of the farmer. Visible only from above it is a technique used in more recent years by the makers of those "mysterious" corn circles to create all sorts of designs.

However, Mr Marks took greatest exception to the way in which we treated his young calves one day.

Someone had seen one of those newsreel films of the famous Calgary Stampede rodeo and it didn't take long, with a few "dares" thrown in, to discover that a half-grown calf is about the nearest thing to a bucking bronco any boy is likely to experience in Britain.

We had bets for marbles on who could stay on longest, once we'd all had a chance to get the hang of it, and for a wild half hour we were real cowboys in the Old West.

The rules were pretty simple. You chose your calf, chased it round the pen until you cornered it against the rails, then leapt astride—like jumping onto a moving bike without using the pedals.

Easy.

From that moment on it was just a question of hanging on the creature's neck with both hands, legs clamped round its ribs, and trying to stay put on the bony back as the calf reared and bucked its way around the pen and your friends, in chorus, shouted out the seconds.

As you were shot off the counting stopped and after two or three goes each we were going to elect a rodeo champion rider.

But, as usual, a miserable grown-up (in the burly shape of Mr Marks) ruined our fun, cut short our competition, and chased us out, all the time shouting about police and setting the dogs loose and various forms of painful punishment as we made for the cover of the nearest wood.

We found, over and over again, that farmers did have this strange habit of becoming annoyed whenever they saw young people enjoying themselves in the countryside.

But back to our egg nesting tale.

There we were, creeping stealthily, or as stealthily as one can creep on a bright summer's day, through the farmyard.

Colley was the one who saw it.

"It" was a hen's egg, a real white hen's egg, nestling under the granary which was right beside the path.

Perhaps "nestling under the granary" is a little too poetic because in fact it was lying, part buried, amid countless years of accumulated farmyard rubbish and chicken droppings.

In the days before the words "free-range" were invented, all farmyard chickens simply wandered about the property, living off what they could pick up and laying their eggs, sometimes in nesting boxes provided, more often in the hayloft, barn or any other sheltered spot they could find. And it was quite exciting—if one got the chance—to help look for farmyard eggs each day.

Every farm, then, had dozens, sometimes hundreds, of hens of all shapes, sizes and colours scratching around the place. A few farms, thank goodness, still do.

This farm was no exception and the granary beside which we now stood was quite obviously a favourite meeting place for the farmyard fowl population.

It was one of those real old wooden granaries, built of overlapping planks (clinker-built a boating man would say) running parallel to the ground, heavily coated with thick pitch that bubbled in places in the midday heat.

The roof, steeply sloping to the ridge, was hung with moss-covered red tiles and the whole structure stood about eighteen inches (that's 45 centimetres in modern speak) off the ground, supported on double rows of great stone "mushrooms".

You can see these "staddle stones" today lining the driveways of posh houses but they were originally designed to stop rats climbing up into the granary in their efforts to get at the grain.

A rat in a granary will spoil much more than it devours by emptying the contents of its bladder and digestive system everywhere, a habit that can result in the deadly Weil's Disease, often fatal in humans.

The egg was beneath the very middle of the granary.

'Who's going under then?' Colley wanted to know.

The question was greeted with an enthusiastic silence.

No-one, it seemed, was eager to crawl into a position from which it might be difficult, or even downright impossible, to extricate himself in a hurry should old Marksy or one of his hired lackeys appear—an eventuality that was far from unlikely as we were in full view of the farmhouse itself only twenty yards away across the yard.

In fact it was something of a miracle that we hadn't already been spotted and hastened on our way.

Then there was the dirt, the dust and several generations of chicken droppings.

Not altogether surprisingly, a democratic majority agreed that Tony was the one for the job.

'But I can't. It's too low'.

'Don't be daft. There's tons of room, even for you'.

'What about the filth?'

'Don't be daft. It's dry filth, it don't smell'.

'What if old Marksy comes?'

'Don't be daft. We'll keep watch won't we?'

His protests brushed so casually and callously aside, Tony, after glancing apprehensively about, got down on his hands and knees and began his unenviable crawl under the granary.

We kept our promise by keeping watch. By some mysterious stroke of luck old Marksy failed to appear.

Tony, meanwhile, his elbows and knees making peculiar tracks through the inches-thick layers of dust, dirt and don't-know-what, was easing his way ever closer to the egg.

'Got it!' he called.

'Come on then. Get a move on. Get back out here before old Marksy comes'.

It was too big to put in his mouth with any comfort so, holding the egg gingerly in one hand, Tony crawled back out, making more elbow and knee tracks in the debris.

As his head appeared from under the granary, Colley bent down, took the egg from his sweaty grasp and held it up for us all to inspect.

'Great!' we chorused.

Tony eased his bulk out from the filth mine and stood up. Then he tried to dust himself down. We all unconsciously stepped upwind as a cloud of grey-blue dust was shaken out of his socks, trousers and jumper.

Even after his clean-up he still looked as though he had been crawling around in the filth under someone's granary.

Of old Marksy there was still, unbelievably, no sign.

'Who gets the egg?' Tony wanted to know.

Although the first egg of just about every other species of British bird had already been "bagged", as was the custom through our usual system, no-one had thought to claim the first hen's egg.

Colley looked around the circle of faces.

'Let's go,' he said.

We sauntered casually past the big farmhouse.

At least we tried to saunter casually. I suspect to any watcher we appeared to slink furtively. I know that I felt about as casual as a fox that's been caught in the henhouse with feathers in his mouth. At any moment we expected to hear old Marksy's dreaded roar.

But the peace of that beautiful day remained unbroken as we left the farm buildings behind us, clambered the farmyard gate and hightailed it for the comparative safety of the far hedgerow.

Negotiating a hole in the hawthorn, we paused in the shade of the far side of the hedge, out of sight from the farm, to inspect our prize more closely.

The egg was large and white, a real nice one, but there was still a difficulty over the ownership.

Colley reckoned that the one who saw it first should have it.

That was him.

Tony said the one who fetched it should have it.

That was him.

We all said that if we hadn't kept watch, nobody would have had it.

The solution, when it came, was a simple one, as usual.

We would share it.

We all agreed that the egg should be cooked as soon as possible and divided among us. We were all getting peckish anyway.

And ten minutes later we were entrenched in a clump of trees at the riverside. Someone found a rusty old tin can, one that we had probably used before as a makeshift crayfish trap. It was battered and grubby but it was watertight.

It was soon filled with water from the stream and our egg placed inside.

Matches were produced, a fire was lit. We used dry grass to start with, then dry, dead twigs and finally thicker boughs fed the flames.

'Make sure there's no damp wood,' ordered Colley. 'Or the fire will smoke like hell and we don't want every nosey bugger in the country knowing where we are'.

We did our work well.

Very soon the campfire was flaring away, crackling merrily and sending up just a thin straight plume of almost transparent blue smoke into the still summer air.

The intense heat from the blazing wood shot sparks and ash skywards, the ash drifting down lazily again , like a miniature snowstorm, to settle on our heads and clothes as we sat in a circle around the flames.

To anyone outside the wood the signs of the fire would be all but invisible.

The old tin containing our egg was placed carefully into the middle of the fire, a task only accomplished at the cost of a singed cuff on Colley's jacket as he struggled to position it with one hand while shielding his face from the heat and fumes with the other. Eyes asquint, he finally got it right.

In a very short time the water in the little can was bubbling furiously, sending our egg bobbing and rattling around its perimeter.

We had no watch so our egg wasn't timed. In any case we had agreed it should be hard boiled to make division easier.

We sat and chatted over the events of the morning.

How sharp-eyed Colley had been to spot the egg.

How ridiculous Tony had looked from behind while he was crawling about under the granary.

And, most wondrous of all, how we had outwitted old Marksy by pinching one of his eggs from under the very windows of the farmhouse.

'Snatched from under his nose!' as Colley put it.

About half an hour must have passed before we decided our egg was ready.

The old tin was eased out of the now-dying embers with the help of two sticks. And, gripped between the sticks the tin, with boiling water, egg and all, was carried to the river and dunked in.

In seconds the egg was cooled and brought back to the fireside.

And there on the grass we gathered round for the ceremonial share-out.

It was Colley who tapped it carefully on the edge of a large stone that had been dredged out of the shallow river bed for the purpose.

We crowded closer, eager not to miss our share. The shell parted.

And, quite suddenly, Colley stood alone, though not for long.

In a flash he had dropped the egg and joined us in a disgruntled group ten yards away.

'Phew!'

'Cawgh!'

'Ergh!'

‘It’s bad!’.

And it was.

Not just ordinarily bad but exceedingly and almost unbelievably bad.

The whole inside, cooked solid, was a sickly green colour. The smell was unbearable.

The egg, in common with most of the other accumulated rubbish under the granary, must have been there for years.

And I didn’t put it past old Marksy to have planted it there deliberately for us to find.

That, of course, would account for the strange fact that he hadn’t appeared when he could so easily have caught us in the act. He was probably at that very moment sitting at home in the farmhouse, laughing his head off.

We put the fire out, left the egg lying where it had fallen, half shelled, in the grass, and trailed off on our quest for fresher fare.

Later that summer we discovered another source of farm eggs.

The hens, ducks, geese and a few turkeys at the next farm over from Marksy’s had got into the habit of laying their eggs “wild” in a hedgerow a full field away from the farm itself.

Just as well, for this farmer was already in our bad books for owning a pair of the most evil-looking crossbred dogs.

For some weeks we visited the “egg hedge” almost daily, collecting a goodly variety and sharing them out at a safe distance from the farm.

But, as with most things, it was all too good to last.

Somebody blabbed. And within just a few days half the kids of the village were trekking to our egg-strike and prospecting for free meals.

With more and more egg-seekers arriving by the hour there were fewer eggs to go round. Often a trip would be quite in vain.

Hardly surprising, then, that the farmer, noticing the remarkable increase in delinquent activity on his property, took to running his dogs loose across the fields at all times of the day—and night—as we discovered when we tried a torchlight search one evening.

Finally, the geese that laid the golden eggs, as well as the hens, ducks and turkeys, obviously tiring of the constant interruption of what should have been a very private activity, stopped laying in the hedge and the bonanza was over.

Ah well, all things must pass.

Meanwhile another hedge on another farm was discovered to be the only barrier between us and a different source of edible booty and it was to this new problem that we next turned our attention.

9: A HOLE IN THE HEDGE.

TO my mind there's a world of difference between scrumping and thieving.

Admittedly our modern complex legal system makes no such distinction and that's a shame.

Because with the disappearance of these subtle differences has gone a certain amount of respect for the Law.

Time was when a lad caught scrumping would receive, and deservedly so, a smack under the ear from the owner of the orchard or even the local bobby.

He would respect this system of instant justice far more than the paraphernalia of irate parents or prosecution, courses of action far more likely to turn him towards a life of crime than any other.

Today a policeman dare not raise a finger to a miscreant or, indeed, even lay a hand on his collar, for fear of accusations of police brutality or assault.

How much simpler life seemed to be, and more enjoyable too, when we either got a pocketful of apples for nothing or a dressing down from Pc Crank.

What I could never understand, anyway, was why a farmer should become so angry about a few apples being nicked off his trees when hundreds lay rotting on the ground.

One farm orchard we knew was guarded like a prison camp.

Although only a hundred yards from one of our favourite meeting places at the village recreation ground, it stood impregnable against a series of scrumping attempts.

That is, until Ripper and I made a "home run".

The orchard, which was separated from the "Rec" by a single meadow, was several acres in extent and was surrounded by a thick thorn hedge.

The farmer, knowing how close the village children played to his precious fruit crop, had had years to perfect his defences, thickening and layering those hawthorns until the hedge was more like a living wall of needle-sharp spikes.

Ripper reckoned that the best time to get in was at dusk, when we couldn't be seen from the farmhouse which stood at the lower end of the orchard.

Oh yes, and there was also the dog.

The dog was a fearsome black creature of the crossbred, uncertain parentage variety favoured by farmers. and habitually slept on the step outside the farmhouse back door, overlooking the orchard.

It was common knowledge among we youngsters that the dog would devour anyone caught scrumping in its master's domain.

I asked Ripper about the dog.

He gave me a knowing wink. 'They tie the bugger up at night, don't they?'

It wasn't intended as a question but as a statement of fact. I accepted it as such.

First, though, we had to find a way in.

A reconnaissance of the hedge in daylight confirmed our worst fears. It was just about impossible to get through.

We were about to give up the whole idea when at last we found a spot, a good way from the Rec it's true, where the thorns near the hedge bottom seemed just a little less dense than in most places.

We stuck a small piece of white paper in the hedge, just above the intended access point, and retired to wait for darkness.

As the late summer evening faded and gave way to darkness we crept silently back across the field towards the orchard, found the paper marker and were soon kicking, poking and elbowing at the lower part of the hedge.

'Not so much noise,' croaked Ripper in a stage whisper as I got a stick into the tiny hole we had so far managed to produce and started rattling it from side to side. 'You'll wake the bloody dog up and it'll start barking'.

With a little extra caution we continued our work and managed to enlarge the gap still further. After a while Ripper got down on his hands and knees, stuck his head through the aperture, writhed from side to side a few times and struggled through.

He knelt in the gloom on the far side of the hedge.

'Come on,' he hissed. 'It's all clear'.

Down I got. I had always had a bigger frame than Ripper so it took a while and a few more wriggles before I had widened the gap sufficiently for me to follow.

Ripper was already at the lowest branches of the nearest tree, reaching up to pick the apples and stuffing them inside his shirt.

I found another tree close by which afforded the same ease of harvesting.

Then we moved quickly from tree to tree, searching for the biggest and easiest fruit to take.

Ripper was away to my right somewhere and I could hear the sound of creaking boughs and rustling leaves, interspersed with his chuckling, half-muffled laugh as he stripped apples from the drooping branches.

I, too, was stretching up, reaching on tip-toe from the dew-wet knee-high grass to grab at apples seen only as dim silhouettes against the darkening sky.

By now, with about two stones of stolen apples in my shirt I had taken on a Billy Bunter appearance.

I was beginning to think about suggesting to Ripper an orderly retreat when suddenly there came a flash of light across the orchard.

A door banged and there were shouts.

Long black shadows were cast eerily through the trees as figures emerged from the rectangle of brightness that was the now wide open farmhouse door.

Much more serious was another sound.

The sound we had hoped we wouldn't hear that night—the barking of the fearful dog.

We were well and truly discovered.

With apples banging around my ribs I raced for the hedge. I was quick but Ripper beat me to it by a stride.

By the time I found the hole in the dark he was already on his hands and knees and half way through it.

The shouting grew louder.

Ripper seemed to be taking an age to get through the hedge.

'Hurry up, for Christ's sake!' I gasped.

'I am bloody hurrying,' was Ripper's response.

At last he was clear and as I dropped to the ground to follow him through I could hear the rapid thud of his feet and the swish of the grass, the sounds receding unbelievably quickly, as he made his escape into the darkness.

And there was a rapid thudding in my chest.

The barks. The shouts. The flashing lights. And the distinct possibility of getting caught were all now closer than ever as I got my head through the hole in the hedge.

It was then I discovered why Ripper had taken so long to get through.

What had been a difficult task getting into the orchard a short while ago had become an absolute impossibility getting out again, laden as I was with a bulging shirtful of apples.

'Oh sod!' I wheezed aloud.

But it was no use. I was stuck.

There was only one thing to do—if there was time.

All those lovely apples that had been so happily stuffed into my shirt a few minutes before were now being tipped out again even more gladly.

Out they came, chucked onto the ground, shoved into the hedge bottom, pushed anywhere that would get them out of the way.

It was only seconds in time but it seemed like hours as that great brute of a hound closed in from behind.

In my mind I could already feel its dreadful fangs sinking themselves into that part of my anatomy that still protruded into the orchard. And I could feel the hard sting of the farmer's stick across my rear.

Unbearable pain. Capture. Humiliation. All seemed inevitable.

But at the very moment I thought my Waterloo must arrive I suddenly found that enough of the illicit cargo had been jettisoned.

A final heave and I was struggling through.

Free!

Not daring to look back I was away across the field in the darkness, head down, legs working like pistons, as I put some distance between myself and my would-be tormentors.

I have since mused that the sensation of fear, properly harnessed, could be very advantageously employed in the world of sport. The country that first successfully develops a "fear drug" in tablet form is surely assured of a good clutch of gold medals at the next available Olympics.

On second thoughts, I suppose it's already been done!

Safe at last in the lane I joined my accomplice. I was puffing like an old steam train.

'What kept you?' he asked.

'I didn't think you'd be so frightened of an old dog!' I replied as calmly as my heaving lungs would allow and with a brave attempt at nonchalance.

In Ripper's front porch, by the dim glow cast by the hall light through the tiny pane of frosted glass in the front door, we sorted our spoils.

Ripper had some beauties. A couple of dozen or so, juicy, red and ripe.

I discovered that, after abandoning most of my loot in the panic to escape, I had been left with only three.

And they were all cookers!

'Look at this,' I moaned, eyeing my friend's pile with envy. 'This's all I've got left'.

'That's really tough,' agreed Ripper. 'Still, if you would insist on staying behind to stroke the dog…'

It was a few months later, just a week before Christmas in fact, that we decided to try our luck in a similar raid.

Only this time the prize was to be mistletoe instead of apples.

Now mistletoe, unlike money, DOES grow on trees, sprouting in big, spherical bunches from the upper branches of a wide variety of host trees.

One of its main problems, regarding picking, is that it likes to grow particularly on thorn trees so that, although it's not necessarily very high it's almost impossible to climb up to.

But Ripper knew a place, only a stone's throw from his back door, where mistletoe was growing on nearly every tree in sight.

Some trees had so many bunches of the stuff sprouting from their branches that they appeared to be in full leaf in the middle of winter.

And as well as being plentiful, the mistletoe there was growing, not only in thorn trees, but on the boughs of much more friendly species like sycamore and lime.

All this was within an area of parkland extending to no more than twenty acres, literally on our doorstep.

There was one problem—there always is—it was private.

Not just normally private but very private. To the extent that there was a thick hedge, backed by a barbed wire fence, all round the property and a whole array of notices saying such things as "PRIVATE" and "KEEP OUT" and "TRESPASSERS WILL BE PROSECUTED".

In addition there was "old Fred".

Not that Fred was that old. It was just that he was an adult which made him old to us.

He was the sort of warden of this estate.

He could run very fast (as we had found out on earlier occasions) and he had a nasty habit of smacking you on the ear if he caught you wandering over his "kingdom", the site of an ancient ruined castle, which naturally attracted us from time to time.

As Ripper's garden adjoined the property it was not altogether surprising that he had been discovered in there many times before. He and old Fred had indulged in many a race for the hedge, all of which, so far, Ripper had won.

Old Fred and Ripper were what you might call arch enemies.

It was with all this in mind and with some trepidation that I agreed to accompany him on this latest raid.

We were to pick as much mistletoe as we could carry, then try selling it for a few pence a sprig around the village to get some extra pocket money for Christmas.

We entered by one of Ripper's favourite secret bolt-holes, revealed when he dragged a large piece of brushwood away from a nice boy-sized gap at the foot of the hedge.

We wriggled through, under the bottom strand of the wire fence and made our way boldly through the paddock towards the trees.

'The important thing is to keep a proper watch out,' said Ripper.

'Old Fred's a crafty bugger. He won't shout. Just creep up on you and grab you. He can run pretty fast but if you see him first and get a good start you can beat him to the hedge easy'.

With this consoling information it all sounded simple enough. Almost too good to be true.

Ripper knew the layout of the land about as well as old Fred did and had a good idea about where to start.

Mistletoe, when it's been growing in the same tree for a number of years, gets old and woody. The leaves are more yellow than green and it doesn't produce so many berries. Eventually the bunch seems to outgrow itself and sometimes dies off.

Mistletoe in this condition is not attractive at all and wouldn't make much cash when we tried hawking it around so we knew what we were after.

Ripper knew the very place. He chose a sycamore tree with a single large bunch growing in it. It was a relatively young growth, nicely dark green, covered in a mass of almost translucent little round white berries.

An ideal Christmas decoration that, divided into couple of dozen sprigs, would make us a quid or so.

And the tree was in a fairly open spot which was also important. It meant that old Fred might see us more easily than if we'd chosen a more secluded place. But if he happened to be on the prowl we would see him from a good way off, giving us plenty of time to get out of the tree, gather our pilfered mistletoe and head for the hedge.

In addition, the bunch was not too high and the tree was easy to climb.

'You keep watch down here,' said Ripper. 'I'll go up the tree, pick the mistletoe and drop it down to you. And for Christ's sake keep your eyes open!'

I was relieved.

It was safer down below. Not only that, I can't stand heights, never could. Two rungs up a ladder and I get dizzy.

So Ripper, whistling casually in his usual tuneless way, went aloft. In no time at all he was twenty feet above the ground and had reached the mistletoe bunch.

'I'll pull it off and chuck it down. You try to break the fall a bit, save the berries coming off,' he instructed in a dramatic stage whisper.

Then, whistling, he commenced the job of harvesting the crop.

Very carefully, so as not to damage it, he broke off large sprigs of mistletoe from the growing bunch and began dropping them gingerly to the ground.

Down below I pranced about trying to catch the falling pieces as best I could.

I stacked them neatly to one side where I wouldn't step on them.

The bunch was even bigger than it had looked from below and Ripper was sending down some really fine mistletoe.

We already had a fair pile mounting on the ground and there was still quite a bit left up in the tree.

I busily did some sums in my head. At a shilling a sprig I reckoned we'd make at least a quid each.

Ripper was till whistling as tunelessly as ever and I was intent on catching the falling mistletoe when some inexplicable sixth sense made me turn suddenly to my left where, to my utmost horror, I perceived the figure of the dreaded old Fred bearing down on us silently at a rate of knots.

How he came to be so close without me seeing him I shall never know. Perhaps it was my preoccupation with counting up the cash. Anyway Ripper's last words to me came shouting back into my memory—"keep your eyes open".

Ripper was right. He was a crafty old sod, he hadn't made a sound.

Fred was a small man and wiry, standing only about five feet three or four. He had a sort of a perpetual pinched look to his face, as if he'd just sucked a lemon by mistake, deep set eyes which seemed darker than they really were, and black, spiky hair slicked straight back, although a few strands stuck out sideways.

He wore one of those dark worsted waistcoats with the pointed fronts, the sort with a shiny silk back and little buckles on shorts straps at the side which were dangling loose as he ran.

The other thing I remember thinking at the time was that what they said about him was true. He could run fast!

I let out a strangled kind of cry.

'Look out Rip. It's old Fred!'

Then I was away like a gamekeeper's whippet.

As I had discovered on more than one occasion, fear lengthens the stride considerably and I reached the hedge in near-record time, cleared it with one mighty leap and was fifty yards across the next field before I risked a hurried glance over my shoulder.

What I saw halted me in my tracks.

Fred had stopped. He was right under our mistletoe tree. And Ripper, whose tuneless whistle still carried faintly over the park to where I stood, was unconcernedly continuing with his picking and dropping the mistletoe to the ground at Fred's feet.

It was obvious that he had no idea that anything was amiss.

I crept cautiously back to the hedge and stood on the safe side, watching.

Powerless to offer assistance I waited. After a time Fred's voice boomed out loud and clear.

'All right you young bugger. That'll do!'

Ripper almost fell out of the tree in surprise and fright and there followed an awful silence as he took in the scene below him.

Old Fred stood at the foot of the tree. It was clear that Ripper couldn't stay up there indefinitely and old Fred looked as though he was prepared to wait all day—and all night if necessary—relishing the thought of capturing his old enemy in this way.

After about twenty minutes of silence Ripper came slowly down the tree and was grabbed by old Fred.

I strained to hear what was going on after he reached the ground. He and old Fred appeared to be deep in conversation or, rather, old Fred was holding forth at length while Ripper stood with his head bowed.

Then came the expected sentence and punishment.

I winced as the sound of old Fred's leathery hand coming into contact with Ripper's ear echoed across the meadow.

Then Ripper was coming my way. Fast.

He came through the hedge, stood up panting and covered the side of his head with his hand. The ear on that side glowed redly.

We watched as old Fred collected up all our hard won mistletoe and headed back towards his cottage on the far side of the estate.

Ripper turned on me.

'Why the hell didn't you tell me he was coming?' he yelled.

'But I did. Didn't you hear me?' I answered feebly.

To this day he still won't believe that I didn't just take off without warning, leaving him up the tree to face the music on his own.

Our humiliation was complete the following day when, making our way along the lane that passed old Fred's cottage on our way to some escapade or another, we saw a sign stuck in the hedge beside his front gate.

On a rough piece of board was chalked the legend "Mistletoe For Sale".

The old walnut tree that stood in the middle of the field opposite Brown's Farm near the village school has gone now. Sadly felled to make way for a big, posh new house.

But it was, in our day, the scene of some of our most daring daylight scrumping raids.

The lane which took us to and from school ran past the front of the farmhouse—which was in reality not a farmhouse at all but a big privately owned house.

The field in which the walnut tree stood was on the other side of the road.

It didn't take us long to find out that the tree was just within range of a well-thrown stick, launched from the side of the road outside the hedge.

And the most exciting aspect of this situation was the fact that the tree was in full view from the owner's front room windows.

At the time of year when the walnuts were ripening and falling from the tree, quite often assisted by marauding rooks, the "walnut run" became a regular feature and it became almost a matter of honour to try to grab a few nuts on the way home from school each afternoon.

This was the drill.

On leaving the school's front gate you made your way as quietly and unobtrusively as possible along the lane. There was, after all, no point in letting the owner know too far in advance that another raid was imminent.

As you went, you collected a couple of stones, a stick, or any other missile that might serve to bring a few nuts to the ground.

At the appropriate spot you walked smartly up to the hedge, took aim and let fly your "nut cropper", trusting that it would strike a part of the tree where the walnuts, now with the familiar wrinkled brown shells peeping through the splits in the rapidly-darkening green cases, grew most prolifically.

All the same, because of the distance from the thrower to the tree, it was a bit of a hit or miss affair.

Sometimes the stick would fall short or miss the tree altogether. Occasionally you would manage to hit the tree without knocking any nuts down. Then again, sometimes half a dozen would come showering down.

Wherever it went and whatever happened you didn't have time to wait and see. The sound of the stick crashing into the thick foliage was usually the signal for the owner to stand up, look out of his window, realise that the blitz was on again and head for the front door.

Your task was to get to the tree first so you set off as soon as the ground-to-air missile was in flight.

Over to the gate.

Get over it.

Race for the tree.

Only twenty yards but it all took time.

You probably didn't see where the stick finished up but you would hear whether or not you had scored a hit. If you were very quick getting over the gate you might even just see the nuts fall among the thickening carpet of brown leaves in the long grass.

About five seconds of scrabbling among the leaves was the time you had to find what you were after. If you hadn't found any nuts by then it was too late.

If you managed to grab up two or three it was your lucky day. Then it was a dash back to the gate.

This is where it all got interesting.

If the owner had come out on cue he was now half way up the front path of the house on the other side of the road.

It needed strong nerves to race at full speed towards him but that was the only way out, to beat him to the field gate, vault it and be away down the lane before he had the chance to cross the road and grab you.

If you did mistime your run, and he beat you to the gate, you had two options. You could turn sharp left and hope to force a way through the thick hawthorn hedge further down the lane (a painful experience) or about turn and try to make your escape on the far side of the little field which was bordered by a dried-up nettle-grown canal bed (just as painful).

The "walnut run" was not a particularly rewarding activity but it did serve to keep body and mind fully alert.

Just about anything of any use was considered fair game for scrumping. I've had brussels sprouts and carrots from the allotments, watercress from Browny's cress beds, strawberries from the back garden of the Railway Cottages and swedes from old Marksy's farm. I even once had rhubarb from the next door neighbour's garden.

On one occasion I arrived home with a whole sheaf of newly-harvested wheat under each arm from a cornfield where I had been sent to glean.

In the days before the modern combine harvester the corn was cut by a reaper and binder (usually called "the binder"), a machine originally pulled by a pair of shire horses but by my day normally towed by a tractor.

Although it looked like a cross between an old-fashioned mangle and a mobile windmill, the binder was in fact a marvellously contrived mechanical contraption.

Its various moving parts, all very noisy, were driven by one huge drive-wheel being pulled over the ground somewhere in the middle of the monster. It could cut the corn, tie it into arm-pit sized sheaves and throw them out in a neat row as it progressed around the field.

All this activity, you will not be surprised to learn, resulted in a good many individual stalks of corn, complete with ear of grain, being scattered about the stubble of the harvest field.

These stray straws were often carefully and laboriously gathered—or gleaned—one by one, by groups of women and children. They could then be used to feed the hens, providing a very valuable and free source of food at a time when many cottage gardens housed a few laying pullets.

Some thrifty farmers went over the newly harvested field with a tractor-drawn hay rake to avoid waste. One elderly farmer even put his two even more ancient spinster sisters to work at hand gleaning.

I very soon discovered, however, that gleaning was not only a long, slow and boring job. It was also very back-aching.

What was much quicker, I found, was to sidle off to a quiet corner of the field, find a shock (stook if you prefer, we always called them shocks) that was one of the little tent-shaped pyramids of sheaves stood up by the farm workers to dry, and heave a couple of the sheaves over the hedge when no-one was looking.

I could come back and collect them from the next field later when the farmer and the other harvest workers had gone in for tea. Safer still, I could wait until nightfall.

For a time we kept rabbits in the garden.

Their homes were an oddly-assorted array of wood and wire hutches built from any odd materials we could beg, borrow or steal.

It all started off with a single pet doe which was mated with a friend's buck, an event that was treated as something of a social occasion and which was watched with avid interest by about a dozen of our chums and acquaintances.

After that things seemed to get a bit out of hand, so to speak, as our pets started breeding, well, like rabbits, and we had to keep building new homes for our rapidly increasing rabbit population, using whatever we could lay our hands on.

What had started as a pleasant hobby, with one rabbit which needed just a few handfuls of greens every day, turned into something of a nightmare as far as catering went.

In the days before processed and packaged rabbit feed (or at least before we had heard about it or could afford it) we found it quite good fun to spend a few minutes each evening picking the dandelion leaves, mixed in with cow parsley and hog weed for a bit of variety.

But as the rabbit family grew, so did the food consumption. Soon it became necessary to carry our foraging further afield. And it took longer and longer to find enough so that most of the evening daylight hours seemed to be taken up in a desperate hunt for greenery.

Then we had a stroke of luck.

Only half a mile from home, up the footpath and over the little iron footbridge that crosses the main railway line, we found that Farmer Rampton had the most marvellous field of lush clover, a favourite rabbit food—as any bunny will tell you.

The footbridge made an excellent access point and would also provide us with an escape route should we be disturbed by anyone coming along the farm track which bordered the field.

For a few glorious days our rabbit food collecting was easy. Five minutes was all it took my older brother and me to rip up great handfuls of the stuff and fill our sack with it. And how our rabbits loved that clover.

Farmer Rampton, in common with most agricultural men in the locality, was known by us to strangle any children who trespassed on his land.

I know that I, for one, always felt very sorry for his own brood of four children, having to have a farmer for a father although, in retrospect, they seemed to thrive on it.

Anyway, a very careful watch had to be kept.

This was made absurdly easy by the fact that Farmer Rampton invariably rode a bicycle. And when he wasn't riding a bicycle he was driving a pony and trap.

Either way, he never went anywhere quietly.

The pony and trap could be heard on the rutted and stony farm track at least a quarter of a mile away, while the bike, which rattled like a lot of tin cans on a string, could be heard, if anything, at an even greater distance.

In later years I often thought that it was odd for a farmer to ride a bike. But ride one he did. I don't believe he owned a car.

One evening, as we filled our sack with succulent clover, backs bent to the task, we were suddenly startled by an awful shout.

We straightened up with a jerk. We were standing no more than twenty yards from the "emergency exit" of the footbridge but there on the lane, 'twixt us and the bridge, stood Farmer Rampton supporting in one huge fist his dreadful bike.

Our retreat was blocked.

He was looking at the fairly extensive area of hard-cropped clover that lay between us, already a sorry sight after several evenings of regular raiding.

'What the bloody 'ell d'yuh think yer up to?'

We didn't really need to answer. It was obvious from our nearly-full sack.

'Rabbits' food'.

My brother choked out the words. I was too terrified to utter a word.

Farmer Rampton surveyed us.

He was not a tall man but he was as broad as a barn door and heavy with it.

His almost bald head was streaked with wispy strands of hair of palest ginger. His arms, too, thick as tree branches, were covered with ginger hair. He wore a collarless shirt with several of the buttons missing. More tufts of hair, more grey than ginger, poked from the gaps in his shirt front and from above the neckband.

His hands were enormous. Easily big enough to strangle us both. Simultaneously.

He wore a pair of dark brown cord trousers, which had obviously seen better days, held at the waist by an ominously thick leather belt with a big buckle. They were tied just below each knee with twine. Heavy boots peeped out from beneath his tattered trouser bottoms.

The bike was just as impressive.

An old-fashioned upright ladies' model with no crossbar, it was covered in red rust. Both mudguards were held in place with string and several spokes in each wheel were missing.

Other spokes that had broken were twisted around their neighbours to stop them fouling the frame as the wheels went round. The front brake mechanism had been modified—the gap left by a lost rod had been spanned by a length of baling wire.

How it bore his weight and, more to the point, how it had got him to his present position without us hearing a sound, will remain forever a mystery.

The thought flashed through my mind, in that instant, that he must have carried his bike to creep up on us like that.

'I'll give yuh bloody rabbits' food! Come on over 'ere!'

The rasping voice sent shivers down our spines.

Our time was up. We were about to be strangled. We had been caught red-handed and there was no escape.

Meekly, with heads downcast, we went to our doom.

Farmer Rampton let go of his bike and it fell with a rattling crash to the stony surface of the lane.

He strode to meet us through the remains of what had once been a nice crop of clover, reached out and took the sack from my brother's shoulder.

At the same time he took my brother's ear between the thick thumb and forefinger of his other hand. Then he turned and led him away down the bumpy track.

I followed in silence.

At the corner of the clover field we stopped.

Farmer Rampton handed the sack back to my brother and briskly ordered him to tip its contents over the fence.

He did so.

In the next field were some black and white heifers which, seeing the activity, had, with the inquisitiveness of their kind, come over to investigate. They immediately began munching at the nice pile of hand-picked clover.

Farmer Rampton took the sack away from my brother again.

'This'll come in 'andy,' was all he said.

In return he handed my brother a hefty smack on the ear which sent him reeling. I stood motionless and open-mouthed.

'Now bugger off! And don't let me catch you 'ere agin,' he warned.

We needed no urging to bugger off which we proceeded to do with the utmost alacrity. Neither did we need the warning about coming back. There was no chance of that. We reckoned we got off lightly just by not being strangled.

Having in my time been a reasonably active and, at times moderately successful, scrumper I sometimes feel a twinge of sadness when I realise that things will never be the same again.

Some of the best orchards that we knew have long since disappeared, the victims of property speculators, with little access roads running in to little estates built on the backland.

And with the vast increase in general prosperity, more pocket money for youngsters, and an almost total absence of youthful hunger, has also died that spirit of adventure which led us into our daredevil raids.

In its place has come the polythene-wrapped pack of imported golden delicious from Tesco. Only half the taste and none of the enjoyment.

Scrumping is not the only rural pastime to become a casualty in the last half century.

Many other traditional country pursuits and pleasures are disappearing, dying with the old men whose skills and knowledge go with them to the grave for want of attention from a younger, uninterested generation.

10: HAMPSHIRE SCAMPI.

MY grandfather, so his daughter, my mother, often told me, used to disappear all night with two friends, a crate of beer and a pack of cards to catch crayfish.

The idea of grandfather sitting beside some stream out in the heart of the countryside at dead of night, playing cards and quaffing ale by the light of a lantern, always appealed to me.

And it intrigued me too.

From a very early age I wondered what it was that, half a century before, had sent grown men out into the darkness to seek the "Hampshire Scampi".

The crayfish is described in the dictionary, quite simply, as "a small, lobster-like freshwater crustacean".

It must also be one of the most mysterious of our native wild creatures—and currently under serious threat from an illegal immigrant. The much larger and more aggressive signal crayfish from north America, brought to Britain to be commercially farmed for posh restaurant menus, is rapidly taking over the habitat of our native crayfish, in much the same way as the grey squirrel, another misguided introduction from America, has all but driven out the native red squirrel.

The native European crayfish used to thrive in many streams and rivers throughout England and as long as anyone remembers had been caught for the table by country folk.

Even the officers of the occupying forces of the great Roman Empire looked upon our crayfish as a delicacy. And yet almost nobody I speak to has even heard of them.

Even fewer have ever seen one—while the number of men who know how to go about catching them in the traditional manner must now be very small indeed.

So I count myself fortunate to have learned the secrets of this ancient country art from a pair of masters, men who, in their turn, were taught by an earlier generation.

It is now many years since my tuition began and my tutors were probably two of the very few people who could lay their hands on the necessary equipment.

On my very first expedition (and there have been many since) I quickly came to understand the urge that sent men like granddad scurrying off into the night, beer and all!

Crayfishing was, in the early part of the last century, fairly common in the south, especially in Hampshire and neighbouring counties where the clear waters of the southern chalk streams seemed especially to encourage these little lobsters to flourish.

In fact trout fishermen liked to see evidence of crayfish which are basically scavengers and do a meticulous clearing-up job of anything dead in the river. Then they make a fine meal, especially when young, for really big trout. On top of all this they are pretty susceptible to any sort of water pollution so that their presence in the river is a good indication that the fishery is healthy and clean.

My two teachers on that first occasion were Bill, a veteran of over half a century of crayfishing and Chris who, although some years younger, had been at the sport since he was a boy, learning from, among others, my own grandfather.

Between them they certainly knew a thing or two about crayfishing and had some stories to tell about it as well.

It was old Bill, now, alas, many years in his grave, who described to me the excitement of the annual crayfishing outing laid on by the local engineering works at which he was an apprentice.

'We'd all meet up,' he said. 'Family and friends and all, and they put us in a charabanc.

'They took us off towards Newbury way and we finished up on a big estate where the company had connections.

‘We had the works band and all along.

‘Some of the men would light a big fire beside the river while the kids were sent out to gather wood. The women would prepare the food, then, as it got dark, the men with the nets would start fishing.

‘The band began to play and there was dancing round the fire. Everyone had quite a bit to drink—it’s a wonder nobody ever fell in the river. The crayfish would be cooked on the spot and eaten with the rest of the picnic, more like a midnight feast!

‘The courting couples managed to wander away from the light of the fire a bit. Yes, our annual crayfishing party resulted in quite a few Spring Weddings.

‘One way or another!’

And he winked.

All that has changed now.

Since old Bill’s days the crayfishing waters have mainly passed from the great estates and become exclusive and closely guarded trout fisheries leased by wealthy syndicates who don’t take kindly to rowdy midnight parties.

And most of the men who worked the nets , like old Bill, have gone.

The crayfish are still there though. They’re more likely to be the American signal variety but they’re as numerous as before—and tasting just as sweet as ever.

My first trip took quite a bit of organising, a lot of badgering and a fair amount of pleading before Chris, whose father, happily, had been a next door neighbour and great chum of my crayfishing grandfather, finally agreed to take myself and a young friend along.

Crayfishing secrets were then still jealously preserved, especially the whereabouts of the few waters where one was permitted to fish for them.

We gathered at Chris's front gate at dusk.

'No use us starting much before ten o'clock,' he confided knowingly. 'They don't come on the feed 'til after the pubs have turned out'.

Generations of crayfishers before us had had cause to marvel at the mysterious connection between the eating habits of the crayfish and the local licensing hours.

I suspected that, long before, closing time had been fixed to suit the crayfish—or at least the crayfishers.

The night, said Chris, was just about right. It was warm and still with plenty of cloud that looked likely to chuck some rain at us before the night was through. And a full moon slid intermittently from behind the big, dark masses of cloud piling up the sky.

In the gathering gloom the moon, momentarily, made the landscape almost as bright as day. Then it was snuffed out again by the clouds to plunge us once more into inky darkness.

Although crayfish, like all coarse fish, are officially in season from June right through to the following March, the fishing is at its height for a few weeks in late summer around Harvest Moon, that mysterious time in September when, for some reason to do with irregularities in its orbit, the moon rises at almost the same time and in the same place on the horizon for several nights in succession.

We were in that critical period.

At last everything was ready. All the gear had been stowed into Chris's ancient Morris and the four of us clambered in. Soon we were on our way.

After a while we turned off the main road down a narrow country lane.

A few more twists and bends and we turned once more, this time into an unmade farm track.

We passed the farm buildings, stopped to open a five-bar gate, waited while Bill closed the gate behind us and then we were bumping our way across a pasture.

The blaze of the headlamps picked up the reflected light from the newly fallen dew which gave the grass a ghostly, silvery sheen. Now and then a rabbit was spotlighted in the beam before hopping sedately into the darkness of the hedgerow.

Another two field gates were left behind us and we bumped and rumbled down a slight slope, rattled over a narrow, rickety wooden bridge, turned sharp left and came to a halt in the long grass beside what seemed to be a reedy, weed-choked stream.

Chris cut the lights but not before they had shown us the swirls of grey mist over the black water of the brook.

We piled out and Chris produced a rubber covered torch. Bill, meanwhile, dug into a rucksack and with a flourish held up his own favourite crayfishing lamp, an antique carbide bicycle lamp made of pewter.

With great care he stoked it up. The sickly fumes wafted over to us as carbide and water met. But eventually he got it spluttering into life with an eerie yellowish flame which gave off the softest of glows, hardly enough to see by, but ideal for its chosen purpose.

Both Bill and Chris were wearing what I found to be was well nigh traditional crayfishing garb—long grubby raincoats, tied at the waist with string, old trousers and gumboots. I was in a duffle coat, jeans and wellies.

Next to appear from the depths of the boot of the old Morris was the pile of fishing gear and I closed in to get a good look. It was an awe-inspiring collection of bric-a-brac.

First the nets. There were six. Each was made from an iron hoop, about two feet in diameter, loosely draped with half-inch mesh string net.

To the iron rim was attached three lengths of twine, each a yard or so long, at equidistant points on the metal hoop. They were knotted at the other end and joined to a longer length of cord which, in turn, ended in a small loop.

You get the idea of what this all looked like if you imagine each net, when suspended by the cord, to represent one of the pans of the scales of justice.

There were also a number of short hazel sticks, sharpened to a point at one end and with a piece of white card stuck into a cleft at the other.

Finally there was an eight-feet long ash pole with a fork at the end.

Then came the bait.

From somewhere in the bowels of the car Chris dragged a plastic bag containing the magic ingredient.

Inside was an assorted jumble of fish “oddments”, mackerel heads, skin, guts and the like, all acquired, at no cost apparently, from a local fishmonger.

As soon as the bag was opened it became abundantly clear that some considerable time had elapsed since the fish had been fresh.

‘Lovely!’ murmured Chris, as we took an involuntary step away from the foul smelling mess in the bag.

‘It’s been out in the sun four days. Just the right time to get nice and fly-blown’.

It was old Bill who took on the unenviable task of baiting the nets. This he did without gloves or other hand covering of any kind, diligently tying a piece of very bad, very smelly fish to the centre of each of our six drop nets.

Then he went and scrubbed his hands off in the stream. It didn’t do much good. Even in the dark we all knew just where Bill was and for the rest of the night endeavoured to stay upwind of him as much as was humanly possible.

Preparations complete we were now ready to start.

Cautiously we followed Chris over to the water’s edge, careful not to shine too much light on the stream and keeping as quiet as we could.

Chris was looking for the first “pitch”.

He soon found a spot where the inky water swirled slowly and deeply under the nearside bank, beneath the overhanging branches of an alder tree. Then he got the first net ready.

This was the moment I had waited for, watching an expert at granddad's favourite pastime.

He took the forked pole in his right hand and the cord of the net in his left, notched the cord into the fork and lifted the baited net clear of the ground, dangling from the end of the pole.

Then the pole, net and all, was swung out over the stream and gradually lowered until the net just dipped the surface. Chris allowed the cord to run slowly through his fingers and we strained our eyes in the dim light of old Bill's carbide lamp as the iron-rimmed net sank slowly out of sight beneath the murky water.

When the net had come to rest on the bottom, Chris took up the slack of the retaining cord and coiled it neatly on the grass. One of the short hazel sticks was put through the loop at the end of the cord and then embedded into the grassy bank. With its white card this acted as both anchor and marker

A few yards further upstream we found another likely looking spot and the process was carefully repeated with the second net. We went through the procedure with the others until all six nets were in position.

'What do we do now?' I wanted to know.

'Well,' returned Chris, with a knowing look at Bill. 'The important part of crayfishing is just about to begin'.

He turned on his heel and tramped off through the drenching, knee-high grass. We followed in silence, line astern, back to the car. From yet another hidden compartment in that vehicle appeared a crate of beer.

I was at last beginning to understand the attractions of this crayfishing lark.

Bill, who had meanwhile conjured up a one-gallon drum of best bitter, said we had to give the crayfish a while to find the bait. And it appeared that the traditional way to pass the time was with a plentiful supply of liquid refreshment.

A groundsheet was spread out on the grass and we settled down. Of old, crayfishers would play cribbage or dominoes but we had too much to talk about to think of playing such games.

Being allowed to take part in the most adult aspect of crayfishing, the drinking ritual, we youngsters felt terribly grown up. We pretended, as best we could, an appreciation of our refreshment as we sipped our brown ales and listened to Chris talking about his past crayfishing experiences.

'It's all a question of being lucky with the timing,' he explained.

'Sometimes you think you've got it just right, on the right night, and you finish up with nothing. Then once I was out in a helluva thunderstorm and we took two sackfuls in less than three hours'.

I ventured to suggest that **I** wouldn't fancy being out in the middle of nowhere at dead of night in a thunderstorm, crayfish or no crayfish.

Soon it was time to make the first inspection of our nets.

As we made our way to the first marker stick the moon broke through the clouds and bathed the water meadows in an eerie glow. I felt like admitting that I wasn't exactly overly keen on being out at the dead of night in any case.

We crept stealthily up to the first marker.

Getting the net out of the water, I was to learn, was even more important than getting it in. It is the whole secret of crayfishing, spelling the difference between success or complete failure.

We watched as Chris, dramatically moon-lit, eased the fork of the pole along the net cord which he had taken up in his left hand again.

He inched his fingers delicately down the cord, the forked pole now disappearing beneath the water. All the time his left hand was taking in the slack in the cord.

When he was ready he gave a good long, steady pull on the cord. At the same time he deftly raised the pole clear of the water. The two actions together combined to bring the net up quickly out of the stream. As soon as it cleared the surface Chris lifted the pole higher and in one easy move—at least it looked easy from where I stood—swung the net safely onto the bank.

'You must do it quickly. But don't hurry,' Chris had said. It had sounded crazy at the time but watching how it was done I realised just what he meant.

As the net swung in, the torches, and four pairs of eyes, focussed upon it.

The dripping mesh was empty.

'Well I'm buggered,' was Chris's comment.

We moved on and net number two came up. Nothing again.

'Don't say it's going to be one of those nights!' said Bill.

We trudged on along the bank once again. The recovery process was repeated and up came net number three.

And there they were! The first of the evening. Four crayfish writhing and flapping in the net!

A large bucket appeared and in they went, everyone eager to help remove them from the net before they had a chance to escape into the grass. Both Chris and Bill heaved sighs of relief.

The three other nets produced seven more crayfish between them and they joined their companions in the bucket.

Our experts decided that the nets should be reset in the same positions 'to give them more time to find the bait'. I should have thought that the smell it gave off would have allowed a blind crayfish in a bath of ink to find it!

'I don't think they're properly on the feed as yet,' said Chris. 'It's a bit on the early side. Barely quarter past eleven'.

We tramped back to the car for another drink. On a good night, Chris told me, you could take up to twenty crayfish in one net on a single "pull". Especially if the river hadn't been fished for some time.

'Don't think we're going to see anything like that tonight, though,' he added.

I asked Bill about the nets. Why just have a slack mesh instead of a tight one? Better still, why not have a good deep net that the crayfish couldn't get out of once they were being pulled up?

'You have a tight net and those crays will be off that net and gone before you get it out of the water,' Bill explained.

'Then again, if it's too slack, what with the iron rim being flat on the bottom, the mesh would billow away downstream in the current with your bait on it. When you came to pull it up odds are it would go inside-out and the little buggers wouldn't finish up in the net at all.

'No,' he added seriously. 'It's taken generations to get it just right and I reckon we've got it about spot on.

'I reckon with the net just draped loosely on the rim the bait stays within the hoop when it's lying on the bottom. Then, as you pull it up, it drops just that little bit, enough to stop the crayfish getting out over the side too easily.

'Mind you. Once you stop pulling, it don't take 'em long to hop off—as you've already seen!'

More talking and more drinking time slipped by.

Time to inspect the nets again and we filed back to the waterside.

This time all the nets held one or two and another ten or a dozen crayfish went into the bucket.

'That's a bit more like it,' said Chris. 'I think we can move the nets now'.

Ten yards beyond the last position of the "first run" we started again. Laying the first net, moving on upstream, laying the second and so on until all six nets were back in the water in new positions.

By now we had travelled nearly a hundred yards from "base camp" at the car and I realised why so much beer had been stockpiled. All this trudging to and fro was going to be thirsty work.

At twelve o'clock more packages came out of the car.

Cold cooked sausages, tomatoes, cheese and pickles, bread rolls.

Terrific!

Washed down with more beer our midnight feast had a peculiar, unreal air about it, though nonetheless enjoyable for all that.

It was then that I took time to inspect the catch more closely.

The bucket was now nearly half full. The creatures inside moved endlessly in their scraping, scuttling efforts to escape. It made a weird and rather creepy sound, echoing up from the old galvanised bucket.

Dark brown in colour, with eight legs plus a pair of businesslike pinchers, the crayfish were exact miniatures of their marine cousins, the lobsters.

The biggest seemed to be about six or seven inches long, from the tip of its outstretched pinchers to the fan-like end of its flapping, segmented tail. In the main, though, they seemed to average about five inches long.

We had caught smaller ones during the evening, one only a couple of inches in length, but these Chris and Bill had tossed back into the water 'for another day'.

Peering at them over the rim of the bucket by the light of Chris's powerful torch, I was fascinated.

Until now I had been a bit backward when it came to taking the crayfish off the nets.

Bill and Chris did it with barely a second glance but I was wary about the pinchers on some of the big "granddaddies" as Bill described the larger ones.

'Only two things you have to remember,' said Chris. 'Hold them from behind, on the wide part of the back, the other thing is that they're pretty slow. As long as you look sharp you won't get nipped'.

I practised with one of the smaller ones that Bill took out of the bucket for me.

I soon found that when holding it as instructed I was surprised by the strength of even the junior crayfish as it flipped and flapped its tail in an effort to break away.

But as long as I held it tight it was quite unable to reach my hand with those pinchers.

It kept swinging them out and up but they wouldn't reach behind its back to where my fingers were. After that I happily handled even the largest.

'Mind you, they **can** give you quite a nasty nip,' said old Bill. 'I was out with my uncle a good many years ago and we had a youngster along for the evening, just like you are. While we were talking he got one of the granddaddies out of the bucket and held it up to uncle's ear without him seeing.

'It took hold of that ear and uncle had a hell of a job trying to get it off. Bled like a stuck pig, he did.

'It was the last time **that** boy ever went crayfishing!'

I also wondered why they were only fished for at night. Chris said that during the day the crayfish hide in holes in the muddy parts of the bank below the waterline, or in thick weed beds and under sunken logs and big stones.

It's only at night that they come out to forage for all sorts of goodies on the river bed.

Another pleasant waiting period elapsed. More food, more drink and more chat. The night began to take on a mellow atmosphere as we sat in the darkness and listened to Nature's noises of that late summer night.

Somewhere, far off, we caught the hooting of a tawny owl, probably having finished its supper, declaring the boundaries of its territory.

Nearer at hand were a mixture of noises, the babbling of the nearby stream, occasionally the rustle of some nocturnal prowler. Stoat? Hedgehog? Rabbit? making its way through the vegetation.

Back at the nets once again, Chris said it would be a good chance for me to try my hand at pulling them in.

With some trepidation I eased the fork of the pole down the cord. Then, with a mighty heave, I hoisted the net out of the water.

For a moment the whole combination began to wobble and dark objects could be discerned dropping off the mesh and splashing back into the stream as I wrenched the pole round to bring the net to dry land.

Miraculously two crayfish had somehow managed to survive the trip and were still on board. They were quickly transferred to the bucket.

At the next attempt I was a little over-enthusiastic. Getting the net cleanly out of the water I swung it smartly up and over the bank.

There was a dull thud, quickly followed by a groan, which was followed even more quickly by an extremely rude word.

The heavy pole had connected with the side of old Bill's head.

He recovered in double quick time, however, seemingly none the worse for the collision, and even joined in the scramble for the crayfish which had been dislodged by the crash and were now crawling around in the wet grass.

Eventually, though, I did get the hang of it and soon afterwards pulled in a net of twelve crayfish, the record single "take" of the night.

By two in the morning the bucket was almost full, the beer was almost gone, I was almost exhausted. And it was time to go.

We all seemed pretty weary by now, all, that is, except Chris. It was as if he could go on forever.

He had to be at work, on early shift, at six o'clock—yet he announced that if the weather stayed good he was going out crayfishing again the following night.

The gear was rapidly packed away and we were soon bumping and jolting our way back to civilisation.

In the kitchen of Chris's cottage the crayfish were tipped into the big, square, glazed stone sink and given a good rinsing in several changes of clean water. While this was going on an enormous pan of water was coming to the boil on top of the gas stove.

When it was boiling the crayfish were scooped out of the sink and straight into the pan, all alive, followed by a handful of salt.

'That's the bit I don't much like,' admitted Chris. 'But it's got to be done. At least they're dead the second they hit the water I suppose'.

I was disturbed by the faint, high-pitched whistling and squeaking noises coming from the boiling pan but Chris assured me it wasn't the crayfish screaming in agony. Just tiny pockets of air in their bodies expanding in the heat and escaping through chinks in their shells, he told me.

Putting that number of crayfish in the pan had put the water off the boil and it was another ten or fifteen minutes before it began to bubble once again.

All the while old Bill was busy with a big ladle, skimming the frothy scum off the surface.

As the water began to boil again Chris looked at his watch.

'Just three minutes now,' he said.

Then they were ready.

The water was strained off into the sink and the crayfish were tipped onto the top of Chris's big white-scrubbed kitchen table.

There were nearly two hundred of them—all now cooked a brilliant red.

Chris showed me how to break the crayfish apart, which pieces to eat, what to avoid. Because of their size, none of them exactly amounted to a feast but the best bits were the tail, properly separated from the brittle pieces of shell, and inside the claws, which I found I could crack open with my teeth before sucking the meat out.

To be quite honest though, at that hour of the morning I didn't feel very much like eating anything.

It was a different story at tea time later that day, however.

Chris had given me a couple of dozen to take home in a bag and with the benefit of eight or nine hours sleep behind me I sampled again my share of the “Hampshire scampi”.

Eaten cold, with just a dash of pepper, brown bread and butter.

Delicious!

Don’t, however, get the idea that the best of rural pleasures occur only after dark.

Night time in the open air has always held fascination for many countrymen, me included, but that other most traditional of English country sports, foxhunting, is purely a daytime pursuit.

11: ON FOOT AND ON HORSEBACK.

WHENEVER the hunt met at the pub near our cottage, which it did a couple of times every season, I was there to watch and admire.

There is something awesome about the sight of a man or woman in tweed and topper sitting astride a great, gleaming hunter, both horse and rider turned out to perfection. It is a sight which never fails to fill me with admiration.

And when the hunt moved off I followed on foot, always keen to see a good chase.

Invariably the huntsman took his hounds up a narrow track close to our cottage to draw a wood called Bell's Copse, always a favourite place to find a fox.

The wood adjoined the main London railway line on one side at a point where it ran through a deep cutting and I, with knowledge aforearmed, always made my way to this railway bank to watch.

On the far side of the cutting was another large wood called Hodd's Copse and what took place between Hodd's and Bell's, as the two were nearly always jointly described, had become something of a ritual.

First the huntsman "drew" Bell's. From the top of the railway embankment you could hear him calling the individual names of his hounds, urging them to ever greater efforts to find the fox, as he made his mounted way down the ride through the centre of the wood.

Quite suddenly would come the single, short "aughroo", the deep voice of one of the pack which had caught the tiniest whiff of fox.

At least we knew that "Charley", as country folk—especially hunting people—called the fox, had been in the wood that morning.

The sound came again, followed by silence.

Yet again, this time a second hound joined in.

Silence again.

Then a more urgent baying from three or four hounds simultaneously.

Charley was still in the wood!

Almost as one the whole pack suddenly gave tongue, the forty-odd throats producing a tremendous echoing chorus of sound that sent tingles up and down my spine.

Charley was on the run and the hounds were on his track.

The baying of the hounds grew louder as they followed the scent of their fox on his traditional run towards the railway.

The huntsman and some of the more regular hunt followers were even able to distinguish the distinct voices of some of the different hounds, although they were mingled in the general noise.

All at once a red-brown form emerged from the undergrowth of the wood at the top of the railway bank.

Without a hint of hurry or worry the fox popped nimbly through the narrowly-spaced wires of the boundary fence and, almost casually, pausing once or twice to look around, made his way down the steep slope of the cutting.

At the bottom the fox paused again, looking first one way and then the other, before hopping up and over the first set of shining metal rails. Four tracks of these he had to cross to reach the far side, at each jump his magnificent brush waving arrogantly in the direction of his pursuers, whose baying was getting ever closer.

Then he was away up the far bank at no more than a trot, through the fence at the top, his tail giving a final flourish as he disappeared into the protective thickets of Hodd's.

The voices of the hounds grew louder as the pack approached.

Then they appeared, first one, then a second, then a few more until they seemed to be streaming out of the wood in endless numbers.

At the railway fence some of the hounds managed to struggle through, driven on by the tantalising scent of the fox that was now so strong in their nostrils.

Some tried to leap the wire, only to fall back among the brambles. One got his head stuck between the narrow strands and began to yelp in pain.

A hunt foot follower soon arrived at the scene and, standing on one of the lower strands, heaved the next one up, getting the wires far enough apart to free the trapped hound and allow the others to get through behind it.

Within seconds they were pouring onto to the top of the railway bank like water from a burst dam and cascading down the cutting towards the tracks.

This was the moment most feared by the huntsman and his helpers.

Inevitably the hounds lost the scent amid the railway lines where hundreds of smoky, greasy trains a day added their deposits to the odours of the pitch-soaked sleepers.

The hounds checked and began casting around for a new scent, milling around, apparently aimlessly, over the rails, unable to determine which way the fox had gone.

One of the whippers-in, minus his horse, raced up the far bank, calling as he ran, to the spot where the fox had so recently disappeared. Another kept watch, looking anxiously up and down the line for signs of an approaching train, straining his eyes into the shimmering distance to where the rails vanished in a faint haze.

At the first tell-tale smudge of smoke on the horizon one of them would race up the gravelled path beside the rails to try to slow the train down. As he ran he would strip off his hunting pink jacket (so named in spite of the fact that it's bright scarlet) and wave it frantically like a warning flag to the driver of the engine. But this time the tracks were clear and the pack was called up the far bank to the fence, put into Hodd's where, in moments, they found Charley's line again and took up the chase with renewed vigour.

The hunt servants and followers heaved a sigh of relief.

But this stage of the game was far from over yet.

The baying of the hounds grew fainter as they followed the track of the fox in a great arc away from the railway cutting and into one of the thickest parts of the wood.

Then, it seemed, they were coming closer again as the fox completed almost a full circle and reappeared, bold as brass, quite suddenly from the wood only a few yards from the place where he'd gone in!

As the voices of the pack grew louder Charley calmly hopped back through the fence, trotted down the embankment, crossed the rails, climbed the other side, popped through the wire at the top and disappeared into Bell's.

The whole chaotic procedure with the hounds was repeated and they were assisted back into the chase by the anxious followers to take up the hunt once more.

This ritual was sometimes repeated two or three times before the hounds managed to press the fox close enough to persuade him to break cover on the far side of the wood and begin a more traditional chase, or until the huntsman decided not to risk the railway line again and called the pack off to try another covert.

But Charley was not always so successful and would occasionally be forced to make a run for it across open fields much sooner.

In this case the hunt followers, on foot and on horseback, others in cars and even some on bicycles, would let out a great chorus of "view hallos" to indicate that the fox had gone away and to give the hounds a line to make for.

When the whole pack was firmly onto the scent, and hunting well, the Master of Foxhounds led the charge of horses in pursuit—the fox, the hounds and the riders between them creating a spectacle that for centuries has epitomised the whole concept of English country life.

Following the hunt on foot was not always as difficult as might be imagined.

The wily fox often went quickly for cover in another wood and by the time the hounds had got him on the move again he could be heading back in the direction from which he had just come.

My most successful hunting day didn't result in a fox being killed but I did finish the day with a handsome profit.

I was trotting along, on foot of course, behind the huntsman as he took the pack down a thick hedgerow towards a notoriously "foxy" wood when suddenly a rabbit, which had been crouching in a "squat" in the long grass, took it into his head to bolt for the safety of the hedge—and ran full tilt into the middle of the pack of hounds.

Needless to say this was suicidal and he didn't get very far. One snap of a pair of strong jaws left the rabbit dead on the grass, the huntsman calling the hounds off to make sure they didn't squabble over the corpse.

I reached the rabbit, which was still twitching in its death throes, and picked it up.

A quick inspection showed me that apart from the fact that its neck was broken it was untouched—except, of course, that it was dead.

Fine.

As I trotted along I took my penknife from my jacket pocket, sliced a hole in the rabbit's back leg between the hamstring and the bone and threaded the other leg through, snicking through the tendon behind the foot to keep it in place.

Then I paused for a while to find a suitable hiding place, finally hanging it up in the ivy covering the trunk of a sycamore tree in the hedge. I would come back for it later.

That was Sunday's lunch taken care of!

I hurried to catch up with the hunt.

A short while later the hounds “found”, as expected, in the wood and disappeared on the line of a fast moving fox.

The riders, who had been taken off by the MFH to wait quietly in a field corner, now came careering down the side of the field towards where I stood leaning on the top of a five bar gate which led into the next field.

I had already half decided at this stage that I’d trekked and chased around quite enough for one day and was just preparing to sit and watch whatever there was to be seen from an improvised seat on top of the gate.

The mounted followers now took up the chase with gusto and from my gate-top vantage point I had a magnificent view as the leading riders put their horses at the hedge and sailed over in fine style, only yards from me.

Then one more portly and elderly gentleman, obviously deciding that cutting a dash for the benefit of the many lady riders was no longer for him, made for my gate.

I hopped down and moved nimbly out of the way but he made no attempt to jump the gate as I had expected him to do. Instead, he leaned down from the saddle, undid the spring-loaded catch and swung it open before trotting sedately through and taking up the chase again in the next field.

I stood by the gatepost as a few more tail-enders followed him through.

Last to go by was a lady rider. In hunting it seems there’s no such thing as ‘after you, madam’.

She was a bony, red-nosed woman, her face, I thought, looking not unlike that of her horse which, in its turn, was a big, gangling, clumsy-looking animal. It didn’t surprise me that she was the last one through.

As she passed she called out to me in a voice that could be heard all over the county.

‘Wod yuu maind clusing the geet’.

It was more of an order than a request and I gave a grudging acknowledgement of the invitation with a thumbs-up sign, swinging the gate closed at the same time.

As I fastened the latch the woman called out something else that I didn't quite catch and tossed something towards me.

It fell into the grass by the gate, gleaming brightly in the wintry sunshine.

Sixpence!

That's more like it!

Very nice, I thought to myself as I picked up the coin and stowed it safely into my trouser pocket, first making sure that it was the one that didn't have the hole in it.

After a few minutes, during which all sight and sound of the hunt vanished, the voices of the baying hounds came faintly across the countryside once again.

And they were coming closer!

Charley had doubled back , crafty devil, and was headed back for the big wood.

The noise of the chase passed by on the other side of a long belt of trees, not many yards from where I still stood and started getting fainter again.

Meanwhile, the mounted followers had reappeared in my field and were galloping back towards me, retracing the route they had so recently taken.

Again the brave ones in the vanguard cleared the hedge at full stretch while I, anticipating the need, unfastened the gate and swung it wide open.

Relief showed clearly on the faces of a few more souls as they changed direction slightly and thundered towards me, sweeping through the open gateway in a grand parade of flying clods and creaking leathers into the next field and away.

'Thenk yu'.

'Thenk yu'.

'Gud show!'

And suddenly there was a miniature shower of coins cascading at my feet as they went by.

I picked them all up.

There was quite a nice collection of sixpences and a couple of shillings beside.

I shut the gate again.

Now whether that fox thought he was working on a commission basis I don't know. All I do know is that hardly had I had the time to count my new and unexpected wealth when the hunt came hurtling back into view once again!

This time I waited until the leading riders were well in view and could quite clearly see that the gate was closed before making a great show of running to the catch and repeating my "gateman" trick, swinging it wide with a flourish.

And this time all but two of the riders headed for the gap, now, after quite a hectic gallop, looking so inviting.

They were more spread out now and took much longer to pass, some right down to trotting speed.

I stood with my best angelic "helpful" look fixed on my face, holding the gate wide as they rode by.

I was beginning to get the hang of things.

'Thenk yu'.

'Gud show!'

'Thenk yu'.

'Thenk yu';

And once more I was rewarded by a shower of coin of the realm for my trouble.

I closed the gate again and carefully collected my booty.

I began to have wistful visions of this lark going on all day and me finishing up with a fortune.

Alas, it was not to be.

The whole procession of fox, hounds and riders finally vanished for the last time that day, leaving me both richer and wiser.

A very successful day.

I headed for home with eight shillings and sixpence in my pocket (equivalent, at that time, to very nearly six weeks' pocket money, a small fortune to me) as well as a nice fresh rabbit at my belt, for which I might be able to cajole another sixpence from my mother.

Yes. A very successful day indeed!

Once a year the local hunt held its point-to-point races in the parkland of a big private estate near the village.

This was the day on which the very rich would rub shoulders with us lesser mortals for a few hours of mutual enjoyment.

It was the time, at the end of the hunting season, when followers traditionally raced their horses against each other and against members of neighbouring hunts over a steeplechase course.

In the very early days the riders would simply be required to race between two previously agreed landmarks, or points, often the steeples of churches in adjacent parishes, hence the terms "point-to-point" and "steeplechases".

They would travel by whichever cross-country route they could find so that local knowledge could easily play a large part in success.

Nowadays the point-to-point races are highly organised affairs and run under strict rules but they are still a time for horses—and people—to be on show.

I always went.

Although racing wasn't due to start until 2pm the activity began rather earlier with horse boxes, carrying the entrants, arriving from mid-morning onwards, some from many miles away.

I always had an early lunch and walked to the racecourse, arriving at about the time the earliest of the car-borne spectators put in an appearance.

They came from far and near, in Land Rovers, in Daimlers, in Rolls-Royces and in Bentleys.

These were the "county-county" set who came as much for the social importance of the event as for the racing.

Then there were the hoards who turned up in beat-up old American sedans, rusty vans, old pick-ups and even lorries.

These were the farm workers, rural families and the dealers, hoping to make a few quid out of the bookies.

All mingled freely and those with vehicles jostled amiably for the best positions against the retaining ropes near the finishing line where, under a pair of Union flags, a panel of tweed-suited, bowler-hatted, binocular-carrying judges would soon be assembled on the back of an open farm wagon to decide the winners of some of the more hotly contested races.

From the Daimlers and Bentleys stepped a smart and elegant array of dignified racegoers, male and female, clad in fur, sheepskin, tweed, cavalry twill, suede and leather.

From the vans, sedans and pick-ups clambered a motley jumble of humanity clothed in wool, denim, plastic, worn worsted and rubber.

From the spacious boots of their vehicles the Bentley people produced folding picnic tables which they covered with red and white gingham table cloths and which they then proceeded to load to capacity with cold hams, bottles of Scotch and brandy, cold chicken, jars of pickles, bottles of wine, salads, port and stilton.

All of this, particularly the liquid refreshment, they attacked with the aid of an impressive array of silver cutlery, delicate china ware and cut glass tumblers.

Meanwhile the van gangs, whose countless screaming children were now running riot around the nearest of the racecourse's birchwood fences, were spreading old blankets on the ground and getting stuck in to their cheese and tomato sandwiches, cold sausages, packets of crisps and bottles of beer.

Until now the smart set had been comparatively quiet but with the rapid intake of several large gins and tonics the piercing voices of some of the women were beginning to make their presence known, especially at times when friends hove into view on the horizon.

'Ooh. Dahling. Look. Thah's Deevid and Fionah. Aye say. Coooee!. Ovah hyah! Cahr for a little semthing?'

And they were joined by a few more tweeds and twills at which the babble of voices shouted in conversation increased in volume by several dozen decibels.

It was always a source of wonderment to me that almost all members of the upper classes appeared to be deaf, a disability that became even more acute after a few drinks.

Oddly enough the gumboot brigade was now curiously silent.

The kids had been called in, had responded after the fifth shout, had received appropriate clouts and were now guzzling themselves on a weird mixture of biscuits, crisps, chocolate cakes, sweets and lemonade.

Fat mothers were openly breast-feeding even fatter babies who had, naturally enough, ceased their bawling, and cloth-capped men were bent in serious discussion over the prospects of finding the winner of the first race.

The afternoon wore on and the loud and raucous laughter of the tweedies grew even louder and more raucous. They appeared to be paying little or no attention to the racing.

The gumbooters were growing ever more silent (sullen is probably a better description) as race after race was run with only the smiles of the bookies to show who the real winners were.

I had little success either.

Mainly because I couldn't get a bet on.

'If the ground is soft, look for a horse with big feet,' a knowing punter had once informed me. 'Or one with small feet if the going's firm'.

It sounded logical so I spent some time at the paddock rails, making a thorough inspection of the hooves of passing horses as they were led round.

And they really did have different sized feet!

By the third race I'd made up my mind.

Warrior Chief had the biggest feet I'd seen all afternoon and as the course was a bit on the sticky side following a week's drenching rain, he was the obvious choice.

The bet of the day.

The horse that would carry the whole burden of my two shilling stake money.

Strangely, I thought, the bookies didn't seem to agree.

A horse called Spring Cleaner was the clear odds-on favourite and my fellow appeared to be the outsider of six runners at eight to one.

Lucky for me, I reckoned, the bookies hadn't noticed his feet!

I was already working out my winnings. Eight times two is sixteen and my two shilling stake back made eighteen.

Eighteen bob!

Very nearly a quid!

What an easy way to make money!

The bookies were standing up behind a kind of wooden barrier, their tall blackboards carrying the chalked-up names of the six runners, each with the offered price beside it. Most of the dozen or so bookies, who formed a neat row, were shouting the odds, trying to attract someone to lay a bet.

Seated behind the blackboards were the bookies' clerks who entered each of the betting transactions into a huge ledger, using a strange form of hieroglyphic language understood only by bookies' clerks.

'I'll give you evens the Cleaner, evens the Cleaner,' yelled one, trying to drum up some enthusiasm.

'You're on. A pony evens,' called his neighbour and the first bookie nodded grudging approval, wiping his board clean as he did so for fear of attracting more big bets on the favourite. Taking high risk wagers from his colleagues was not what he had in mind at all.

They all seemed to be offering the same odds.

'Two to one the field. Two to one bar one,' came the shout from one of them.

All this strange language meant nothing to me.

I walked up and down the row, looking at the boards. But no-one was offering better than eight to one on Warrior Chief.

I paused in front of one bookie.

I gazed up at him.

He glared down at me.

He was wearing a dark brown felt trilby hat and thick camel-coloured overcoat, which seemed more or less standard uniform for bookies. In his hand he held a bundle of betting tickets which he kept flicking through like a pack of cards.

He was flabby faced and had a bulbous nose which was coloured by something more than the fresh April wind.

I thought: 'Old grog-blossom'.

But I actually said: 'Two bob win Warrior Chief'.

He looked down at me without moving.

'How old you, son?' came his gruff demand.

'Eighteen,' I lied.

'So's my Aunt Fanny's cat. Bugger off, you'll get me arrested'.

I intended to argue but he wasn't even looking any more.

I looked up once more, hopefully, but he was having none of it.

The sign at the top of his board read "Bert Simmons, London".

You couldn't trust these London bookmakers anyway.

Bert Simmons was now busy serving someone else so I walked disconsolately away, my two shilling stake still clutched in my hand.

Dejected, I made my way over to the start to watch the horses set out on their gallop but I was to get the last laugh after all.

The echoing, monotone voice of the race commentator came tinnily over the loudspeakers.

'Under starter's orders. They're off!'

They thundered away towards the first fence.

'And it's an even break...Going to the first it's Spring Cleaner, Topsy Turvy and Firefly all together...A length back to Make Believe with Bednobs close up...Another length back to Warrior Chief'.

He's holding him back to conserve energy I thought.

'They're at the first now...And there's a faller at the first!...It's...Let's see now...It's Warrior Chief...Warrior Chief is a faller at the first...Meanwhile the remaining five are heading...'

Thank you, Bert Simmons. You saved me more than a week's pocket money.

Horses have always been a major part of my enjoyment of country life—but at a distance. I don't ride. In fact the truth of the matter is that for years I was terrified of horses at close quarters.

And it was all Lushy Smith's fault.

Old Lushy Smith was a gypsy who often left his horse and cart in the road outside the village garage while he went in to pester Bert Goodall for old car batteries and cast-off tyres for which he might get a return of a few bob from the scrap dealer in town.

"Lushy" wasn't his real name and it had nothing to do with his drinking habits which, by all accounts, were also pretty wild. No, his nickname was merely a derivative of his real name which, in true gypsy style, was the good old biblical name of Elisha. Incidentally, his two eldest sons were named Elijah and Reuben.

His cart was a four-wheeled, flatbed affair on which the original wooden wheels had been replaced at some time by metal car wheels with proper pump-up tyres.

A nailed-together wooden bench seat spanned the width of the front and its plank flooring behind was always piled high with a tatty collection of junk of all kinds from rusty lumps of cast iron to bags of woollens and rags, lengths of lead piping of doubtful acquisition and old tin baths.

The paint was peeling from the wagon's frame, revealing glimpses of a remarkable variety of colours underneath.

But if his cart looked a shambles, his horse looked even worse.

It was a pony really, not big enough to be called a horse, and its ragged piebald coat hung on it like an old threadbare overcoat. It must have been all of thirty years old.

Lushy obviously didn't believe in wasting time or energy on grooming the creature which was also liberally spattered with mud and filth where it had rolled on the wet ground. The dirt on the white patches of its hide made it look even more bedraggled.

Its mane was long and matted and its hip bones stuck out from skinny haunches.

Altogether a sorry looking sight, the beast stood impatiently easing its weight from one spindly leg to another. Whether or not it actually had a name I don't know, I never heard Lushy or any of his considerable tribe address it with anything more than a grunt.

One day when the tattered combination of nag and wagon was drawn up at the garage, I happened to be passing on my way to the village shop.

I stepped into the road to go by, whistling as I went, and casting a disdainful eye over the cart and its contents.

As I drew level with the horse it turned its scruffy head to look at me and gave me a baleful stare.

I stared back.

Then, as I turned away to continue my walk, it suddenly thrust out its neck and sank its bared teeth into my shoulder.

Luckily I was wearing a thick jumper and jacket which cushioned the effect of those vice-like jaws. Even so it hurt enough for me to scream out in pain although, looking back, I think it was as much shock as pain.

At the same time I lashed out at the vicious beast with both fists as it attempted to shake me like a terrier shakes a rat.

After a few seconds, which seemed a lot longer, the brute let go and I jumped clear, nursing a badly bruised shoulder.

At that moment Lushy came rushing out to see what the commotion was about. At least, he was shuffling a little faster than usual.

'Wha's goin' on?' he wanted to know.

'Your bloody horse,' I yelled at him angrily, my pride hurt a bit more than somewhat. 'He just bit me!'

Lushy smiled, his few remaining teeth, although yellowing, showing up starkly against the blackness of the gaps where other teeth once had resided. His mouth formed a misshapen opening across the grizzled stubble of his face which clearly had not seen the benefit of water or razor for a week or more.

‘Oh-ah,’ he replied, without the slightest show of remorse or concern for my ravaged shoulder. ‘Ah. ’ee will do’.

And from that day on I have always treated all equines with the greatest distrust.

Horses were forgotten, however, when I became involved in that other great country field sport, shooting.

Not as a participant but as a paid “beater”, a job that soon became my favourite winter Saturday occupation while providing a very welcome regular boost to a personal economy that seemed rarely to balance.

12: BEATING ABOUT THE BUSH.

ON a fine, brisk Saturday morning in early November I met Colley cycling through the village street with what looked suspiciously to me like a rabbiting stick strapped under the crossbar of his bike.

Naturally I wanted to know where he was going.

'Beating,' he replied.

It was a new one on me and I asked him to explain.

The local gamekeeper, it seemed, needed a crowd of men and boys to walk through the very private woods that he had spent all summer chasing us out of!

Not only was he willing to let you tramp his precious territory all day—he was prepared to pay you as well!

'Seven shillings for the day,' said Colley. 'Oh, and a free bottle of lemonade at dinner time'.

It all seemed too good to be true.

The idea, Colley explained, was to drive all the gamekeeper's jealously guarded pheasants and suchlike out of the woods and over the guns that were waiting at the end of the copse. The sportsmen would then shoot them, at least that was the theory, and we would be right on the spot to watch all the fun.

Although a couple of years his junior, and a good deal smaller into the bargain, I begged Colley to take me along.

'What about your dinner?' he asked.

'Don't want any,' I eagerly assured him.

‘What about your mum?’

‘Oh, she won’t mind’.

‘All right, come on then. You can have one of my sandwiches’.

Without stopping to leave word about where I was proposing to go for the rest of the day I broke into a trot beside Colley’s bike and in this fashion we travelled the two miles to the appointed meeting place, the cartshed at Marksy’s farm.

By the time we arrived several others were already there, standing around waiting, a couple of men and half a dozen older boys I recognised from the village.

They wore gumboots, thick trousers, leggings of various materials and designs, ranging from proper oilskins to the new plastic fertiliser sacks, duffel coats or heavy mackintoshes, some tied up with string, gloves, scarves and an assortment of hats in wool, cloth and leather.

They all carried sticks.

More beaters arrived. A few more men, a lot more boys.

At last came the gamekeeper.

He strode into view round a bend in the farm track, a flat tweed cap on his head, a stick in his hand and a spaniel at his heels.

Stan the keeper was tall and thin. Scrawny I suppose you’d call him. His face was gaunt and his nose had a decidedly sharp edge to it. His eyes, by contrast, were a lively, pale blue and seemed capable of looking everywhere at once without actually moving.

Between his lips hung a half-smoked thinly-rolled handmade cigarette which had gone out. In all the years I was to know him the half-smoked home-roll was a constant feature. It wouldn’t have surprised me to learn that he slept with it in his mouth.

As well as a tweed cap he wore thick green tweed jacket and breeks. Thick knit socks, covering the lower half of his legs, disappeared into hefty brown boots.

And when he spoke it was with the most wonderful Norfolk accent.

'Mawnan evvywon,' he said.

'Mornin' Stan,' came the chorused reply.

After a quiet discussion at one side with two of the men, Stan turned back to face the waiting assembly of would-be beaters.

The boys were impatiently kicking at the ends of their sticks or poking at the fragile white layers of ice that last night's cold snap had left covering the water-filled cattle hoof marks in the muddy track.

'Raight,' said Stan. 'I naid fefteen beatahs and fauw stops t'day'.

And he began picking the ones he wanted from the waiting bunch.

Rather, it was more a question of weeding out the few he didn't want. Like me.

'Yo ben beatan' befauw?' he asked me.

'No,' I had to admit. 'But…'

He looked at me. At my shoes. My short trousers. My coatless frame and my stickless hand.

'Yo c'n come back next yeah,' he told me.

Most of the others got a job, including Colley. There was just me and two other diminutive hopefuls who were left behind as the body of men and boys, at a word from Stan, turned and followed him in an untidy straggle down the track and out of sight round the bend to begin their day's beating.

We turned the other way and made our way homeward.

The following year, intrigued by the mystic of it all, I tried again. Only this time I went better provisioned and better equipped.

True to his word, Stan gave me my first job as a stop and for the rest of the season—and many seasons to come—there was no question about where I was going to be on a Saturday.

Each shooting day started the same.

We gathered at the farm cartshed and waited for the keeper. Then one of the men took off to one side several of the smaller boys (at first I was one of them), the number depending upon which part of the shoot's land we were covering that day. They were the "stops".

This little group would "walk in" a number of long and overgrown hedgerows, a job that entailed bashing the hedge with our sticks, some of us each side of the hedge, as we headed for one or other of the far-off pheasant coverts.

Any gamebirds in the hedge were driven ahead of us, some breaking cover to fly towards the safety of the trees, some running ahead of us and creeping across the open ground to the wood.

A boy was left in a prominent position at the end of this hedge to "stop" any birds wandering back into the hedge again before the wood was driven later in the day.

This process was repeated round the extremities of the shoot's property, all the hedges, pieces of rough land and long, narrow belts of trees and scrub being walked in towards the central woodlands.

As they progressed, stops were left in strategic positions, the size of the party diminishing as the work continued, until all the stops were out, at which point the man in charge of them went off to join the main body of beaters.

By this time the others had already completed the first drive of the day at the other end of the estate, the sound of guns echoing across the late autumn air to the stops in their various positions.

Sometimes the stop was "picked up" and relieved of his duty during the morning if the wood he was "stopping" was being driven early in the day's programme. When the beaters came to drive his wood he simply joined in with them and for the rest of the day was a beater himself.

Often, though, it was afternoon before he took his place in the line and, at one particular position, the boy didn't join up with the others until the very last drive of the day.

Several of my friends willingly volunteered to go out as stops, knowing that they wouldn't have to struggle through any brambles or bogs, and when it was cold they could light a little campfire to sit by.

At lunch time the "stopman" had to retrace his steps of the morning—while the other beaters were eating their sandwiches—to deliver bottles of lemonade to the boys still out on their lonely sentry duty.

Personally I found stopping a thoroughly boring job and always tried to avoid it, preferring to beat about the bush and see the action of every drive.

Eventually, when I grew big enough, the keeper never picked me for a stop so I didn't have to try to dodge his eye any more.

Once you were a proper beater you felt really grown up and there was a great sense of camaraderie among the regular gang.

There was also an endless stream of banter and leg pulling which, every so often, especially when we were walking between drives, had to be silenced by Stan's stern; 'Not s'much lahkan about theah!'

At the start of the day we trudged after the keeper to the end of a long wood where we formed up into a line abreast, ten yards or so apart, depending on the size of the copse.

The keeper stood in the centre of his line of beaters and would walk slowly along a ride that ran through the middle of the trees where he could keep control of the entire operation.

At each end of the line, ready to walk down the outside edge of the covert, was one of the older men. Their job was to see that neither side of the beating line got too far in front of the other, or too far behind.

They were known as the flank beaters or "flankers" and, as their job entailed the least physical effort of the day—walking the outside of the wood rather than the bushes in the middle—their title also became the derisory term for anyone who wasn't pulling his weight.

Sometimes two of the "Gentlemen", as Stan called the sportsmen carrying guns, arrived with twelve bores crooked in their arms to walk alongside the flankers.

They were “flank guns” who were to shoot at any pheasants breaking out to the sides or flying back while the drive was in progress.

We stood and waited again while the Guns, usually eight and so far unseen, got into position at the far end of the wood.

For some reason a sportsman in the shooting field, clothed in tweeds, brogues, canvas spats and deerstalker hat, carrying a seat stick on one arm and a double-barrelled twelve bore shotgun on the other, a cartridge bag slung over his shoulder and a Labrador retriever at his heels (and not infrequently accompanied by a bored looking female) is known simply as “a Gun”.

Once they’d settled themselves in the open field beyond the far end of the wood, at specially numbered stands marked by white cards stuck into the tops of a row of cleft hazel sticks, the drive could be started.

The signal to start was a police whistle, blown loud and long, and was given by the head of the shooting syndicate. Stan answered with a short blast from his own, which dangled from a piece of cord around his neck, and shouted last minute orders to the beaters.

‘Awraight. On y’goo. And kaip a straight liyne!’

As one we all plunged into the wood, tapping our sticks on the hazel clumps, bashing the bushes and collectively emitting an unbelievable cacophony of sound comprising innumerable whistles, shouts and tongue clickings.

The secret of being a good beater (and that meant not getting shouted at by the keeper too often) was to keep in line and equidistant from the beaters on each side of you.

Every few minutes you had to check to make sure you hadn’t dropped behind, got in front, or drifted over to one side. And you had to do this in the thickest cover, even though you got only an occasional glimpse of your neighbouring beaters through the undergrowth.

All the while you still had to perform the job for which you were being paid the princely sum of seven shillings (35 pence) for the day, beating the brambles, briars and bracken to flush out the cowering pheasants.

At first the birds tended to run forward when disturbed.

Pheasants are not overly keen on flying, it takes up too much energy, and prefer to leg it out of harm's way or crouch quietly in the bushes, hoping that you will walk on by. Which we often did.

When we got further into the wood one or two would take noisily and clumsily to the air in a crashing of dead twigs and a whirring of wings, the cock birds hooting in annoyance and alarm.

Those that flew out to the side or tried to turn back came under fire from the flank guns, warned by many a shouted 'Back, right' or 'Back left'.

Others flew forward, away from the noise of the steadily advancing line and gained height and speed in their headlong flight for the sanctuary of a neighbouring wood.

These were the birds that would be passing directly over the row of quietly waiting standing guns.

And again the shouts would go up 'Forward, right, forward!'

Whether all this hollering ever served any useful purpose for the guns I have never discovered. But it did give us all a chance to vent our enthusiasm and excitement, as well as an odd sense of self importance. And Stan never seemed to mind.

The nearer we approached the guns the more birds rose.

Those that had run forward during the earlier part of the drive now found they were going to have to fly anyway and from time to time a whole flush of pheasants rose at once, eight or ten birds heading out over the guns simultaneously.

Then the keeper would call a halt to his line with a shouted 'Bide back!' and the order to cut the vocal noise.

'Hold it!' came the message relayed down the line from beater to beater. 'And just keep those sticks tapping!'

We stood still, rattling our sticks between the uprights of the nearest clump of hazel, as pheasants continued to take to the air in front of us. Then the flight would stop and we got the order from Stan.

'Goo on. Steady though!'

A few yards further on we were halted once more as another formation of pheasants took to the air.

By now the end of the copse was in sight and we could see, through the trees, what was happening up ahead.

A cock pheasant, unseen in the brambles despite his vivid red and green and gold and brown, suddenly rose with a great crashing of branches and wings from almost under the feet of a startled boy, the bird's raucous "ca-cawk ca-cawk" echoing through the leafless wood with a somehow metallic resonance.

The pheasant gained height, climbing at a steep angle up through the branches and over the tree tops, then levelled out and with rapid wing beats headed in the direction of the guns at an ever-increasing speed that looked deceptively slow.

'Over. Forward,' came the shout from several eager throats.

The big bird, long tail streaming behind, was flying high and fast as he passed over the end of the wood and, watched by at least a dozen pairs of eyes, crossed the open ground beyond, apparently oblivious of the row of guns standing silently below.

The beaters in the wood watched and waited.

From where they stood it looked as if the pheasant had already negotiated the guns successfully without a shot being fired.

'They've let the bugger go…'

Hardly had the words left the beater's lips when one of the gentlemen in tweeds, scarcely visible through the intervening undergrowth, unhurriedly presented his shotgun.

There was a slight puff of smoke, the flying bird crumpled in mid-air and began to fall. A few small feathers floated from the already dead pheasant as it plummeted towards earth.

Strangely late came the bang of the exploding cartridge which killed the bird. The report was still echoing round the countryside as the pheasant thudded to the ground.

'Good shot!' we all cried out in unison.

We moved on again.

More pheasants were driven up and flew to take their chances over the waiting guns. A few flew on, unscathed, through the barrage of shots, much to the disgust of we beaters whose efforts had put them up to such advantage. Some of those efforts now seemed wasted.

More were shot and crashed, lifeless, to the ground.

At the end of the wood we got the order from Stan to 'Knock them laast few bushes raight ouwt!'

And a couple more birds, which until the last few seconds imagined they had been overlooked, took to the air.

Then all was silent until another long whistle blast was followed by a final, shouted 'All ouwt!' from the keeper.

It was both an order to the beaters still in the wood to get into the field and a signal to the guns that the drive was over.

The beaters stood around for a few moments, discussing the successes and failures both of individual guns and of their own efforts.

Next order was: 'Beatahs this waay!' And we trooped off again behind Stan to make ready for the start of the next drive.

The gentlemen in tweeds unloaded their guns. The labradors, which all this time had been sitting, tails wagging, tongues lolling, whining quietly in anticipation, behind their masters, were now put to work retrieving the fallen birds.

Each, it seemed, knew precisely where the pheasants shot by his owner were lying and in a short time all had been collected and laid out ready for collection by the Land Rover which served as a game cart.

On one huge private estate where I occasionally went beating, those weeks when Stan didn't have a shoot day, they had a proper horse-drawn, canvas-covered wagonette which was fitted out inside with rows of wooden racks, especially made to take a pheasant hung by the neck, but their bag was often several hundred brace a day.

More Land Rovers arrived to transport the guns and their attendants in unhurried and leisurely style to their stands for the next drive.

The beaters had already walked to their positions or, if it was a question of saving time, had been driven there, crowded together on straw bales lined out on a farm trailer towed by a tractor.

And so the drives, and the morning, progressed.

After about five such drives a halt was called and by now young legs were aching and young tummies were rumbling.

We trekked wearily to the keeper's cottage.

The guns and their ladies disappeared inside to partake of a home-cooked country lunch prepared by the keeper's wife, the aroma from which (it was usually something like a rich beef casserole) wafted outside to the hungry beaters who were left to enjoy the delights of their own sandwiches in the comfort of Stan's woodshed.

If the weather was kind it was nicer to eat in the open, sitting on the little wooden bridge that crossed the stream just a few yards down the track below the cottage, or slumped over a pile of cordwood logs outside Stan's garden gate.

Everyone got a free bottle. Beer for the men, lemonade for the boys.

Even the stops, some of whom were still sitting it out in lonely vigil around the countryside, got their share, taken out by the stopman who had to make the rounds during his own lunch break.

And everyone had his favourite sandwiches, brought from home in a variety of shoulder bags, haversacks, carriers, and even in pockets.

Everyone, that is, except Bert.

Bert was the oldest of the beaters, well into his sixties and, naturally enough, a flanker in every sense of the word.

Wherever there was a particularly nasty piece of terrain to negotiate, there was Bert—as far away from it as possible.

If it was rough on the right, he'd take the left. If it was thick on the left, he'd take the right.

And for his midday meal Bert always brought the same thing, the thick end of a fresh crusty loaf into which had been pressed a good-sized pat of butter. With this went a big chunk of Cheddar cheese and an apple, the whole lot wrapped up in a bright red cloth which he produced as a sort of bundle from somewhere about his person.

He would sit, usually on the pile of cordwood, his red cloth spread across his knees. Then he would take an ancient pocket knife from another secret compartment hidden under several layers of clothing, open it, give the worn, slightly curved blade a wipe on his trousers and begin to eat.

The knife, which was the same one he used for cutting sticks and paunching rabbits, was razor sharp. He would slice off a corner of the bread with a deft, inward-curving stroke, scoop a smear of butter onto it and top it with a chunk of cheese, whittled off the large lump with the same swift towards-the-body action.

The combination of bread, butter and cheese was steered mouthwards by the knife blade, aided and guided by thumb and forefinger.

Once safely in it was quickly joined by a piece of sliced-off apple, followed by a mouthful of beer, chewed around together, swallowed and washed down with another mouthful of beer for good measure.

Somehow Bert always managed to wangle two bottles of beer.

In spite of the keenness of the knife blade, we never once saw him cut his finger or, more surprisingly, disfigure his face.

Bert was also good at other things on beating days. Like getting himself a free Sunday dinner.

For a long time I could never make out why Bert, never noted for putting himself out more than he could help, always insisted on riding his bike the extra half mile along the track beyond the meeting place at the farm to the keeper's cottage, just so that he could walk back again with Stan.

It was a bumpy, rutted track at the best of times and, of course, it meant he had to set out from home nearly half an hour earlier than the rest of us in order to make the return journey to the cartshed.

As he reappeared with the keeper someone invariably would make such a comment as: 'Here comes Stan—with his best flanker!'

It was Colley who reckoned: 'He only does it to creep. Brown-nosed old bugger'.

But all the comments were made just out of the hearing of Stan or Bert.

Admittedly his bike, an old upright, black-painted machine, was handy at the end of the day when we had all been paid off at the cottage gate and were making our way back on foot to our own bikes at the cartshed.

But Bert was so slow, and he never seemed to be in any particular rush to get away that, as often as not, we beat him back to the farm anyway.

The clue to the mystery was the carrier on the back of Bert's bike.

It was a simple affair, just a plain metal shelf fitted behind the saddle and over the back wheel. On it Bert always carried an old rolled-up mackintosh which no-one had ever seen him put to use, rain or shine.

But he always had it on his bike 'just in case', he used to say. It was tied on firmly with a piece of string.

During the midday break Bert, having finished his bread and cheese, would carefully fold away his red cloth. Then he would saunter nonchalantly over to where his bike was left propped against the hedge of the cottage garden.

In full view of everyone he would untie his old mac' , unroll it, give it a shake out and stand looking seriously at the sky, as though contemplating the weather. Then with a grunt and a shake of the head, he proceeded to roll the ragged garment up again and tie it once more onto the carrier of the bike.

And it took us literally years to twig that the bundle, once replaced, was always just that bit bigger than when he'd untied it.

In fact never a Saturday passed without a rabbit or a hen pheasant finding its way by perfect sleight of hand into Bert's old rolled-up mac'. Of course, when we finally knew, it became the object of a good many jokes and leg-pulls at Bert's expense.

As we sat eating our sandwiches someone would call out to Bert, who invariably sat a little apart, 'Looks like rain s'afnoon. Better go 'n get yer mac' off the bike!' Or, especially if the keeper or one of the guns was within earshot, 'Wha' cha got fer dinner termorra, Bert? Rabbit? Or pheasant?'

That got his dander up.

'Shut yer mouth. Mind yer own bizniss y' nosey bugger,' he would hiss, hoping Stan hadn't heard.

And we all laughed.

Once at the end of a day's beating he overtook a group of us walking back to the farm for our bikes.

As he wobbled slowly by one wit shouted out: 'Hey Bert! Yer mac's jest fell off the back! Hey, what's that inside?'

And Bert, concerned lest his guilty "secret" be exposed, swung round so quickly that he lost control of the bike and all but fell off into the trackway.

But having recovered his balance, and his composure, and having ascertained that his precious bundle was still intact, he pedalled off homeward with many a muttered dire threat about what he would do to 'you young buggers' next week.

How Bert acquired his booty in the first place was something that had to remain a mystery although, being on the flank, often out of sight of the other beaters inside the wood, he always had ample opportunity.

Especially if there was a flank gun walking alongside him and anxious to get a shot in.

It didn't take much imagination to picture Bert, touching the peak of his flat cap as he took a newly shot rabbit or pheasant off the gentleman in tweeds, and whining: 'Let me take that off you, sir. Give you a free 'and like'.

And the gentleman would gratefully give up his burden.

In the walk between drives it was the work of only a second to transfer the game from his hand into one of the capacious pockets of the big loose overcoat he always wore.

To Bert, a bird in the pocket was worth any amount of birds in the hand!

I have since contemplated that Stan knew exactly what old Bert was up to each week but preferred to turn a blind eye.

As time went on I became more and more experienced in the ways of beaters.

I learned, for example, that if I stuck pretty close to old Bert the odds were that I'd have an easy day. Easier, that is, than otherwise.

One particular drive that none of the beaters looked forward to was "the Moor".

In spite of its grandiose title, the moor was simply a hundred acres or so of rough pasture, water meadow, swamp and bogland stretching down either side of a small stream.

It was criss-crossed with ditches, dykes, drains and streamlets and was never really dry.

In fact there were large areas, where the coarse round-stemmed reed grass grew in great clumps, that were constantly under a foot or so of water.

There was no way round.

You had to go through, ploughing hopefully on and praying all the while that the water wouldn't go over the tops of your wellies—which, of course, it invariably did.

The ditches and streams had to be jumped.

Some were just a couple of feet wide.

Others were wider.

Some were a lot wider and you would have to select a relatively narrow section, go back a dozen yards to get a run, and take a flying leap.

Sometimes you just couldn't jump far enough.

A grunt of exertion would be followed by a loud 'Aaargh!' as a foothold was lost. The shout was followed by a splash and the splash was followed in its turn by a commendable selection of expletives as another poor unfortunate went thigh-deep into the water and black, oozy mud.

Almost immediately a cheer would go up from all those who had witnessed the event, especially from those who had already negotiated the obstacle successfully.

Those who hadn't seen it got the news by a kind of bush telegraph, shouted down the line from beater to beater.

'It's Shaver! He's fell in! Right up to the waist! Christ, you should see the mess he's in!'

Old Bert smiled but kept quiet.

For ages I never understood why he always volunteered to take the longest way round the left flank on the moor. Positively eager he was.

While Stan was still sorting out the details of the drive, Bert would stride off in untypically buoyant fashion with a shouted: 'I'll get a start on and take the left, Stan. Save a bit of time'.

Eventually I discovered that although it meant a long walk near the end of a tiring day (which is why no-one objected to him volunteering) the rough ground under the far hedge was the only place on the moor where you could be guaranteed a dry pair of feet at the end of the drive.

Once discovered, I was quick to appreciate that, at a squeeze, there was room for two on that dry left flank. That's why, when Bert strode off, I hastily followed in his steps with the generous call: 'I'll go too, Bert. On your inside'.

All the effort out on the moor seemed frequently to us to be for minimal return.

About all we put up, apart from the odd pheasant or two ('must have bloody webbed feet,' Bert used to say) were the snipe.

The snipe reminded me of a skinny starling with long beak and legs.

They would rise silently from almost under your feet, to give a once-repeated "twit-twit" once they were on the wing. Sometimes just one or two, sometimes a "wisp" of six or eight would spring up together from the coarse grass and rushes.

And they were fast, reaching top speed in just a few yards.

Once clear of immediate danger from the beaters they gained height rapidly, climbing with a swift zig-zagging flight up against the wind and towards the guns positioned behind a thick hedgerow at the far end of the moor.

By the time they reached the guns they were well up, little more than little darting dots of grey against the greyer sky.

The gentlemen in tweeds had a field day with their effort to bring them down.

It wasn't unknown for close on two hundred shots to be discharged at the snipe between the eight guns, all of whom seemed to be in a tranced, lemming-like and frantic haste to fire their pieces ineffectively into the sky.

At the end of the drive we were lucky to have three or four dead birds to show for the impressive and furious barrage which had left gun barrels almost too hot to hold and a mass of empty number seven and eight cartridge cases littering the ground around each stand.

Occasionally the moor drive did produce moments that made it all worth while.

Like the time that the white-headed and angular figure of the ageing Lord Dorchester rose from a shooting stick seat to bring down, with a right and left, a pair of fast-flying mallards that had looked for all the world to be too tall for the guns to touch.

It's the only time I've ever seen the line of beaters stop in mid-stride to applaud.

I continued my beating activities for many years. Even when I left school and had a regular full time job I made sure not to miss my paid-for winter Saturday sport.

And talking of full time jobs, isn't it strange how you can almost drift into a career?

When I did finally leave school I had not the slightest notion of what I wanted to be, except that I fancied a job in the country.

So when I was offered a three-month summer job on a local farm, I literally jumped at the chance.

13: COWS IN THE CORN.

BARNEY took hold of Mr Stanley's favourite plum tree with both hands and gave it a good hard shake.

A dozen fat, purple shapes thudded down into the grass and Pongo and I began a mad scramble to pick them up before the owner appeared.

This little ceremony had occurred every morning since I started work at the farm the previous week. The tree, hardly more than a bush, had been loaded with plums. Now it was almost devoid of fruit.

At twenty-seven years of age Barney was the senior man on the farm. He drove the tractor, organised the milking and generally lorded it about in the absence of "young Mr Stanley", the tenant farmer.

Young Mr Stanley, a bachelor, was in his late thirties. His aged father had died the year before, leaving him in sole occupation of the huge, rambling farmhouse and its 350 acres. But his heart wasn't in farming.

Pongo was the other farm worker, besides myself, a lad of eighteen or nineteen whose sole ambition in life, it appeared, was to be allowed to drive the ancient Fordson Major tractor.

Sometimes he got his wish.

'We'll take the tractor down t'the river,' said Barney. 'If you fill the radiator, Pongo, I'll let you drive 'er back'.

'Coo, thanks Barney,' returned Pongo.

He got the job quite often as the vehicle's cooling system leaked like a sieve and had to be filled up two or three times a week.

When I'd started at the farm young Mr Stanley took me to meet this remarkable duo, introducing them as "Barney and Douglas".

As soon as he'd left to attend to 'something in the house' (which he did with noticeable regularity) Barney turned to me and informed me, 'We don't call 'im Douglas. We call 'im Pongo'.

'Why do we call him Pongo?' I asked somewhat hesitantly.

''Cos he's a bit bloody daft,' returned Barney.

This, apparently, was all the explanation Barney considered necessary and as Douglas seemed to have no objections I didn't press the matter.

So Pongo it was.

I was a little fearful of Barney if the truth be known. He was likeable enough most of the time and had a big, smiling , open sort of face which belied what often went on behind his startling blue eyes.

For I was to find, soon enough, that he was the teller of the most outrageous stories, a romancer of the first order, one of the biggest rogues for miles around and capable of some pretty doubtful turns of "humour".

I remember he used to play football for the village team (which itself had the reputation of being "robust", to say the least). Built like an ox, and with just about as much ball control, he was the star centre forward and his crashing runs through the middle were legend.

He would rush at breakneck speed, the ball somewhere and somehow at his feet, arms flailing and legs flying, straight for the opponents' goal mouth, clearing a swathe through the defending players, and not a few of his own as well if they were in his path, like a bulldozer run amok.

Those who didn't get out of the way got sort of carried along in the rush, to end up with Barney, the goalkeeper—and sometimes the ball—in the back of the net.

But I'm forgetting the plums.

Since his father's death, young Mr Stanley had let the farm go rather badly. Although not directly responsible for the farm buildings, which were in reasonable condition, all the livestock and the machinery was his own.

And it was all in pretty bad shape.

The farm house garden, too, had gone to weed and seed. The vegetable plot, flower beds and lawns all overgrown with nettles, docks and thistles.

Mr Stanley struck me as being a man not particularly interested in farming but having been born to it, so to speak, was making a brave effort to soldier on without the guiding hand of the old man.

One thing in which he did show an interest was his plum tree.

It seems to have been about the only thing about the place, that he had ever planted, which could be said to be a success. And whatever else on the farm was neglected, the plum tree remained his own peculiar favourite, to the extent that he even sometimes cut the grass around its base.

That was why he was so pleased when, this year, the plum tree looked like turning in a bumper crop. Except that Barney and Pongo and me all liked plums as well and they were fast disappearing.

The trouble was that after we had left our bikes in the cartshed each morning, we had to walk down the path beside what had been the kitchen garden to reach the cowshed for milking.

And the path led us right under the plum tree.

When we'd got our plums, Pongo would go on down to the bottom pasture to fetch the cows while Barney and I sat in the early morning sun, enjoying the fruit and the relaxation.

Mr Stanley used to help with the milking, although he didn't usually appear until most of them were finished. Now and again he would turn up early, just to keep us on our toes, we reckoned.

On this particular morning we heard the bang of the back farm house door while we were still picking up the plums and had just enough time to conceal the booty in shirts and pockets before Mr Stanley ambled into view around the side of an old garden shed.

As it was, we were still standing guiltily around his plum tree as he approached.

‘’Eard you comin’ boss and waited for yer,’ announced Barney, from whom untruths flowed like water from the Niagara Falls.

‘Ah,’ replied Mr Stanley.

Then he looked up at his precious plum tree and wrung his hands.

‘Those bloody birds have been at my bloody plums again. Damned things,’ he wailed.

‘Yeh, don’t they though, boss,’ chirped Barney. ‘Tell you what. If you lend me yer ol’ four-ten I’ll sit out ’ere fer a while at dinner time an’ knock a few o’ they buggers off’.

I gasped at this one.

For days Barney had been trying to find an excuse for borrowing Mr Stanley’s little shotgun.

Three times in the past week he’d seen a cock pheasant sunning itself beside the hedge at the side of the track leading down to the river where he went to fill the tractor’s radiator.

Each time the wily bird had slowly walked off into the hedge as the tractor drew near.

Barney knew that at twenty-five yards he could stop the tractor and bowl that pheasant over easily with the four-ten.

As if to add point to his offer he added: ‘There’s a few rats gettin’ about in the cowshed agen too. Saw one’s big s’cat yesty. Wouldn’t ’urt to ’ave a go at them an’ all’.

I have to admit. He was right about the rats.

Mr Stanley didn’t reply. He just nodded. He was obviously doubtful about Barney using the gun and, I suspect, was a little overawed himself by Barney’s blustering, overpowering manner.

Mr Stanley was hoping that Barney would forget the conversation.

We knew that Barney wouldn’t.

Trying hard to suppress a giggle, Pongo scuttled away to fetch in the cows for milking.

Within five minutes he was scuttling back again, out of breath.

And cowless.

'They've gone!' he announced.

'What 'ave?' Barney wanted to know.

'The cows,' said Pongo.

'What, all of 'em?' asked Barney.

'Yep,' returned Pongo

'Gone? Where to?' demanded Mr Stanley.

'Dunno,' countered Pongo guardedly.

I glanced from one face to another in turn, trying to keep up with this amazing three-sided conversation.

I listened in awe.

The whole herd gone?

Rustlers?

A gang of cattle thieves with a fleet of lorries?

I began to get quite excited.

Which was more than could be said for Mr Stanley and Barney.

They seemed to have heard it all before.

'Have they broken that fence down again?' asked Mr Stanley, exasperation in his voice.

'I didn't look,' replied Pongo brightly.

'Then go and bloody well look, you fool!' yelled Mr Stanley, his exasperation turning to anger. 'I expect they're in the corn'.

Off went Pongo again and we all followed. If the cows had disappeared it would take a while to find them and round them up so we might as well help.

Sure enough, their usual pasture was empty.

Sure enough, the rickety wire fence was broken down again.

And sure enough, there were the cows, belly deep in the young wheat of the next field, munching contentedly.

Perhaps they weren't quite belly deep.

Ample evidence of several earlier visits by the herd showed in the fact that about two thirds of the ripening crop had been browsed off. Most of the rest was trampled beyond recovery.

Mr Stanley's failure to keep the fences in order was costing him dear.

He wrung his hands and rounded on poor Pongo.

'I thought I told you to mend that bloody fence properly the last time,' he wailed.

'I did mend it,' whined Pongo. 'But I couldn't do much with it. We ain't got no tools nor nails nor nuthin'. And the wire's rusty. And the posts're rotten. And...'

'Never mind that now,' yelled our employer, who knew that Pongo was right. 'Let's get the bloody cows out of there before they ruin the lot'.

'Bit late, ain't it boss?' asked Barney sarcastically.

Mr Stanley turned on him, ready to put him in his place once and for all.

But Barney was wearing his big, loveable, disarming smile. Before Mr Stanley could speak he added hastily: 'Just a joke, boss. Just a joke!'

We rounded up the herd, driving them out through the gate at the top of the field and into the yard.

They seemed to go quite willingly, clearly well satisfied with their morning raid on the cornfield.

As the last one trotted into the yard, encouraged by a prod from Pongo's stick, Mr Stanley closed the gate and stood surveying the scene of his devastated wheat crop.

'Look at that bloody lot,' he moaned. 'That's cost me a couple of hundred quid for sure'.

And he wrung his hands.

'Never mind, boss,' piped up Barney. 'Think of the extra milk you'll get!'

Mr Stanley looked at him quickly. But Barney was wearing that big smile again. He was 'just joking'.

The cows streamed across the yard and in at the open cowshed door, each walking straight to its own allotted stall inside. We got on with the milking.

No all-electric, vacuum-operated, fully-automated milking parlour for us. It all had to be done by hand with bucket and stool.

I was still inexperienced then and, consequently, pretty slow.

I found the peculiar hunch-back position on the tiny milking stool made my bottom numb and my back ache. The continual pulling and squeezing made my wrists and arms throb with the effort after only about ten minutes.

Barney, however, milked at high speed, completing about three cows to my one. Mr Stanley was quick too. Not so fast as Barney but thorough. Pongo was slow, as he was at everything else.

Suddenly, from somewhere down the row of quiet animals, came the almighty clatter of bucket on concrete and a roared oath as Pongo was kicked by one of the younger, less docile beasts.

Mr Stanley swore too as he saw the stream of spilt milk cascading down the drainage gutter that ran the length of the milking stalls.

Pongo was rubbing himself where he'd been kicked and vowing never to go near the animal again.

Barney, seeing his employer's temper was at fraying point, called out: 'Leave 'er to me, Pongo. You get on with the next one'.

Barney wasn't going to be put off by a belligerent cow and told her so in no uncertain terms as he made ready to continue the job of milking her.

She was a youngster, one of the newcomers to the milking herd. Already she had established herself a reputation for ill-humour and a couple of nasty cuts on her teats, sustained, presumably, in the escape from the pasture, didn't make her manner any sweeter.

It took her about two minutes to decide that she didn't like Barney any more than she liked Pongo. Her hind hoof came lashing up and then forward and down, missing the milker's head by a fraction of an inch to land squarely in the bucket.

She just stood there, hoof in the milk, refusing to budge while Barney shouted and swore ineffectively.

'What's the matter with you bloody lot,' shouted Mr Stanley. 'Can't anybody milk a bloody heifer? Come out of the way for Chrisakes. Let me see to her'.

Barney, having retrieved his bucket and discarded what milk he had managed to get, was happy to oblige.

Mr Stanley approached the task in a businesslike fashion.

First he tied the cow's hind legs together with a piece of rope, lashing her tail down at the same time for good measure.

Then he positioned the bucket under her udders, turned his peaked cap back to front and in a swift movement, squatted beside the animal, thrusting the stool under his backside as he did so.

With his head buried firmly into her belly he began to milk.

At the same time he looked up at us as we stood watching in anticipation.

'What you waiting for? Haven't you ever seen a cow being milked before?'

We dispersed up and down the cowshed to continue our work.

All was quiet save for the gentle, rustling movements of the cows as they fidgeted from foot to foot, and the soothing "squit-squit" of the milk as it jetted into the buckets.

Time went by without further incident.

Then it happened.

A roar of surprise and pain, coupled with anger, and a clanging and a sloshing sound echoed around the low building.

We all looked up in time to see Mr Stanley sail backwards out of the stall and into the gutter where he made a perfect one-point landing in a nice, soft, fresh cow pat.

The bucket sailed out after him with a clatter and the evidence of his success in milking the heifer showed in the amount of milk flooding over the cowshed's concrete floor.

Nobody said a word.

Neither Pongo nor I would have dared.

But Barney started to sing "Oh what a beautiful morning…" in a loud, off-key voice which was the only way he could keep from bursting out laughing.

Mr Stanley muttered a lot, wrung his hands, and hurried off to attend to something in the house.At the midday break we trooped up to the cartshed to fetch our sandwiches.

Barney stopped at the back farm house door, tapped on it almost inaudibly and, getting no response, lifted the big iron latch and marched boldly inside.

He walked across the stone-flagged kitchen, lifted the old double barrelled hammer action four-ten down off a rack on the wall, picked up a box of cartridges from the big wooden dresser and marched boldly out again.

At the cartshed Barney said: ‘Come on. We’ll go ’n sit in th’ orchard. So’s I can shoot some o’ they birds wot’s bin pinchin’ the boss’s plums’.

Already he had convinced himself that it was, after all, the birds which were responsible for the disappearance of Mr Stanley’s favourite fruit.

In the garden we sat, backs to the shed wall, eating our food. Barney used one hand to guide the bread to his mouth while the other steadied the loaded shotgun that rested across his knees, both hammers fully cocked.

A pretty little male chaffinch flitted into an old apple tree nearby and sat there shouting “pink-pink” at the top of his voice.

Barney raised the gun and squinted along the barrels. Just practising, I confidently assured myself.

There was a sudden violent explosion which made me and Pongo jump and the chaffinch, now a mangled corpse, dropped lifeless to the ground.

I was trapped in a stunned silence.

‘That’s one bugger that won’t eat no more plums!’ commented Barney in triumph as tiny feathers drifted pathetically down.

I hadn’t the courage to argue that chaffinches never eat plums.

The noise of the shot dissuaded any more birds from venturing into the garden and before very long Barney got bored with waiting for something to shoot at.

He stood up, stretched his legs then, quite suddenly, snatched Pongo’s cap from his head, hurled it into the air and blasted it with both barrels.

Barney’s aim wasn’t so good with a moving target and he missed. In spite of Pongo’s whining protests, Barney had two or three more unsuccessful attempts to shoot the hat.

Tiring of his repeated failures, he finally hung the cap on a low branch of the plum tree, stepped back a few paces, raised the gun and let fly.

Pongo's cap danced merrily away in the air as though jerked on a piece of elastic and Barney allowed him to run after it and fetch it.

'Look at me 'at!' wailed Pongo.

We looked.

There was a ragged three-inch wide hole through the middle of the crown.

Barney laughed.

'That's done it good,' he insisted. 'Let a bit o' daylight an' air get to yer brain!'

From then on Barney carried the gun with him wherever he went, taking potshots at sparrows, starlings, blackbirds and even robins.

Oddly enough, although he always had it with him on the tractor, he never saw a sign of that old cock pheasant again. Word had got around, it seems.

Instead he contented himself with stopping the tractor every so often to shoot at anything that moved—and quite a few things that didn't.

Finally the box of cartridges ran out and Barney, unable to find replenishments, reluctantly put the gun back on the kitchen wall rack, much to the relief of Pongo and me. We could now eat our sandwiches in relative peace.

That peace was eventually broken, this time by Pongo, when he got into a spot of bother while attempting to perform a good deed.

We had noticed that for some time one of the scores of scrawny hens that pecked about the yard suffered from a very bad limp and more than once Pongo had mused over what was wrong with it, and whether he could help.

'Leave the bloody thing alone!' was Barney's advice. One day, as we sat eating our midday meal in the cartshed, this poor hen hobbled by.

'I'm goin' ter catch that 'en an' see what's wrong with 'er,' announced Pongo.

Abandoning his sandwiches he rose and started to stalk the hen, which hobbled away as soon as he approached.

After a few minutes it was obvious he was getting nowhere.

As soon as he made a rush for the bird it limped and flapped out of his reach. When he slowed or stopped the hen did the same. Barney and I watched in great delight at this free lunchtime comedy show.

'Take yer jacket off an' throw it over 'er,' called Barney encouragingly.

Pongo thought this was a great idea and peeled his jacket off as instructed.

Then, with the garment held out at both arms length, looking for all the world like a trainee matador, he began the chase again.

Round and round they went, first quickly, then slowly, in a comic *pas de deux*.

Each time Pongo speeded up the hen accelerated her hopalong flight. As Pongo slowed the chicken's pace was reduced to a limp.

Once or twice Pongo threw his jacket hopefully but each time the hobbledy hen easily avoided the trap.

We sat and laughed 'til the tears ran down our faces.

This farce might have gone on all lunchtime had it not been for the appearance in the yard of Mr Stanley's huge old rooster.

The set of his comb, the brilliance of his neck and tail feathers, the length of his spurs and the very way in which he used to strut about the place left no-one in any doubt about who was top cock.

Around the farm yard the cats, and even Mr Stanley's old dog, kept well out of his way.

The big cockerel stood and surveyed the scene in the yard.

Here was some big, lumbering intruder trying to steal one of his wives!

Without more ado the great bird streaked across the yard to the attack.

Pongo didn't see him coming. He was too busy stalking the hen and our chortled shouts of warning came too late.

From ten yards away the rooster took off like a rocket—and landed, in a flurry of flying feathers, flapping wings and scrabbling legs, right in the middle of Pongo's back.

He hit him with such force that Pongo almost fell headlong.

Pongo screeched in fear as the big cockerel flailed away at his back, crowing at the top of his voice.

For a moment we were silent, dumbstruck with amazement at the force and ferocity of the attack.

Then we started to hoot with laughter as Pongo and the big cockerel fought it out.

It wasn't much of a fight.

Pongo kept trying to reach his assailant but the bird clung doggedly to the back of his thick woollen pullover. Finally, Pongo gave in and beat a hasty retreat, scurrying across the yard. At this point the cockerel at last dropped to the ground and gave chase on foot.

The pair of them disappeared from view at high speed round the corner of the cartshed, Pongo still screaming in fright, the bird still flapping and crowing.

After a while the cockerel reappeared alone to strut up and down the yard, stopping every now and then to preen his ruffled feathers and shake them into position before throwing back his head to let out yet another victorious "cock-a-doodle-doo".

The tears of mirth were still running down our faces and our sides were aching when Pongo crept round the other end of the cartshed, sidled along the wall and scuttled into the comparative safety of the building to resume his lunch.

'That damned bird didn't 'alf give me a start,' he said.

Barney obviously thought that was a bit of an understatement.

'Bloody near scared you t'death you mean,' he chuckled.

So the summer progressed and harvest time came round.

Not surprisingly the tractor broke down while we were towing the decrepit binder out of the barn.

That took two days to repair and Mr Stanley wrung his hands.

At last the tractor was got going and the binder was coupled up.

A start was made on harvesting the barley. I say barley because that's what had been planted, so I was told. It looked more like a field of thistles to me.

After two circuits of the barley/thistles the binder broke down and the man called in to fix it took another day to get it working again.

Mr Stanley wrung his hands some more and went to attend to something in the house.

After a few more trials and tribulations the barley was cut and shocked ready for carting and ricking.

The oats followed and then what was left of the wheat where the cows had been.

A gale blew down most of the shocks and we had to spend another three days standing them all up again.

Mr Stanley wrung his hands.

The old wagon was made ready for the carting, with big wooden ladders fore and aft, and to everyone's surprise it all appeared to be in working order.

We stared carting the barley.

They let me drive the tractor slowly along while Barney and Pongo loaded the wagon.

Barney walked alongside, tossing the sheaves up with a pitchfork to Pongo, who rode on the back, arranging them on the wagon, straw butts outwards to stop the load slipping off.

The load did slip off more than once when Pongo didn't get chance to arrange the sheaves properly. This happened because Barney's favourite trick was to heave the sheaves, two at a time, with such force as to try to knock Pongo off the cart. Which also happened more than once.

Mr Stanley stayed at the corner of the field nearest the farm yard where we were building the rick.

He wanted to make sure that, if his employees couldn't load a cart properly, at least the rick would be built so that it didn't topple over.

Each time we brought a wagon load to the rick Mr Stanley would take each sheaf as it was tossed down and place it carefully by hand in the prescribed manner, butts facing out, the sheaves radiating from the centre.

The rick gradually grew. By the time it was about twelve feet tall it was time to use the elevator.

This was a wondrous piece of equipment reminiscent of a moving staircase with rows of spikes instead of stairs, driven by a little petrol engine.

It was raised to the correct angle, the motor started, and the moving tines would carry the sheaves up to the top of the ever-growing rick with the minimum of sweat.

Well, that was the theory.

Only, of course, the elevator wouldn't work. And the engine wouldn't start.

Once again, no surprise since they hadn't been working at haymaking time—and had been sitting out under the hedge in a "nettle shed", unattended and unrepaired during the intervening three months!

Mr Stanley wrung his hands once more and went off to attend to something in the house.

When he returned an hour later he announced that we should have to use a "pitch hole".

I was intrigued.

It entailed building the rick on up without the aid of an elevator by leaving a tiny platform twelve feet above the ground where the rick started to taper off..

One man stood in the pitch hole and as the sheaves were tossed up to him, he pitched them on up to the top on a sort of human bucket and chain principle.

Standing precariously in a tiny, airless pitch hole on a hot late summer afternoon, heaving hundreds of dusty, thistle-filled barley sheaves high over your head with a pitchfork was not exactly my idea of a fun day. But I got the job anyway.

The harvest eventually over, Mr Stanley called us into the farm kitchen and told us in a serious voice that he was giving up the farm and selling up. We weren't unduly surprised.

Everything was to be sold off in one massive "Sale of Livestock and Deadstock".

The day before the sale we lined up all the machinery in a field in front of the farm house. The auctioneer's men swarmed around, sticking numbers on everything they could see that wasn't a fixture, rooting about in the cowshed, barns and outhouses.

Barney said if you stood still long enough they would stick a number on you.

The day of the auction dawned and people began to arrive in big cars. Mostly they were farmers and dealers from all around the area.

They looked over the items for sale and shook their heads.

Then the bidding began.

Within a very few minutes it was apparent that Mr Stanley wasn't going to get very fat on the proceeds.

Nobody seemed to be all that keen on anything. Not enough to pay good money for it. I could only. assume that most of the farmers attending the sale had thrown away better equipment than that which was on offer.

Even the cows didn't arouse very much interest.

When Mr Stanley saw the sort of prices his precious cows were being sold for, he wrung his hands and went to attend to something in the house.

Later in the day, at the back farm house door, he paid us our final week's wages in little brown envelopes, the first and only time he had ever bothered with such a formality.

We stood and watched as he wrung his hands and disappeared for the last time to attend to something in the house.

My farming days were over. And I wasn't too sorry.

'Don't worry,' my mother said. 'Something else will turn up. It always does. When one door closes, another one opens. You'll see'.

And she was right, of course, as usual.

She had always had this uncanny knack of seeing beyond the obvious.

And she was superstitious too. To the point that I considered absurdity.

She was a great believer in fate—and even claimed to be able to foretell the future with the aid of tea-leaves and dreams!

14: BUMP IN THE NIGHT.

IT may be because country people live so close to nature and the natural that they also have such an affinity for the supernatural.

Certainly, superstition seems much more rife in country districts than in the towns and belief in ghosts, spirits and "things that go bump in the night" is, in rural areas, much more widely held.

I, for one, don't intend to scoff.

For a number of years our family lived in a beautiful, picturesque brick and timbered cottage set in the centre of one of Hampshire's loveliest, as well as historic, villages.

Mind you, the price we paid for the "ideal" life was a conspicuous absence of all things now considered to be the necessities of life.

The lavatory, for instance, was a small, ivy-covered construction at the far end of the garden.

We had no bathroom, which meant a weekly dip in a tin bath in the kitchen, with water heated in an old copper boiler.

And the water itself had to be drawn from a communal well thirty yards up the road.

It was while bathing one day, when the rest of the family was out (the only time you could get a little privacy) that I first experienced the strange feeling that I was to encounter many more times in that kitchen.

The big back door, at one end of the kitchen, was a real solid wooden job, an inch or so thick with three wide cross-pieces running horizontally across the inside of it and another two going diagonally between them.

It had two bolts, one at the top and one at the bottom, and an old lock with a key big enough to do justice to a church door.

Before climbing in your bath you had to close and lock this door as neighbours and relatives had the disconcerting habit of walking straight in unheralded.

At the other end of the kitchen were two tall brick steps which led up to a second door. This one led into a passageway and pantry which in turn opened into the main living room through yet another door.

After locking the front door, once again to keep out unwanted visitors, you also shut the interior kitchen door to cut down on draughts, especially in winter.

With all these preliminaries completed you were now ready for the tub.

On this particular day, having shed all my clothes, I stepped into the bath and settled down for a soak.

Then, quite suddenly, I began to get the strongest and most disturbing feeling that there was someone else in the room.

The whole kitchen was only about nine feet wide by twelve feet long and what with the big old kitchen table and chairs, the fireplace, the copper, the sink and, of course, the bath, things were a bit cramped.

But still I could feel a peculiar presence there.

It all sounds now, in the cold light of day and many years later, a bit silly. But I swear I felt the hair prickling at the back of my neck and the weirdest tingling in my back. Literally shivers up and down my spine.

I was facing the big back door and the sensation I had was of someone behind me.

So I got up in the bath, turned round and settled back again, this time facing the door at the top of the steps.

It was no use.

It was still behind me.

Although I knew I was completely alone in the house I spent an uncomfortable five minutes, turning first one way then the other, trying to see who or what was there.

There was nobody.

I kept glancing around that tiny room, looking over my shoulder, but the sensation remained with me.

I reached the stage where I dare not close my eyes, even to soap my face, so I left it unwashed.

Being naked in the bath didn't do much to alleviate my feeling of utter vulnerability.

My bathing was finished in double quick time. I dried myself, pulled on a pair of pants and unlocked the back door.

The sun streamed in and at last the terrible feeling was gone.

But from that day on I could never bring myself to face another bath at home when the house was empty and even washing my face at the kitchen sink sometimes gave me decided palpitations.

No other room in the cottage had this effect although the whole house, being several hundred years old, was forever giving little creaks and groans of its own, especially on cold winter nights when the roaring log fire in the living room hearth warmed the timbers and joists of the upstairs rooms.

Many years later, long after the family had moved to a more modern house, we were reminiscing about the old days in the cottage. With a certain amount of embarrassment I confessed to my older brother my secret fears about the old kitchen.

He told me in a quiet and serious voice that he had experienced the self-same feeling while bathing or washing there.

He had always been too ashamed to say anything about it!

On another occasion at the cottage we were all awakened in the middle of the night by the old piano which was apparently playing all by itself in the living room downstairs.

The keyboard lid was firmly closed and the ghostly playing stopped abruptly the minute we all piled into the room.

This phenomenon occurred on several successive nights.

Then we found that a family of mice had made their home inside after chewing through the back of the thing (it was a pretty prehistoric instrument) and spent each night running up and down along the little hammer connectors, resulting in what appeared to be a novice practising scales.

I know my mother was always convinced that the cottage was haunted.

Mind you, she was one to talk, what with her superstitions.

Black cats, ladders, spilt salt.

A few hundred years earlier she'd have gone up in smoke, burnt at the stake for a witch without a doubt.

Well, she was a bit of an amateur witch on the quiet.

I don't mean that she went flitting around the countryside on a broomstick, wearing a tall, pointed hat. Or that she was cut out for this other witch's caper of dancing naked around a bonfire in the middle of the woods. Blimey! Perish the thought!

No, it's just that, well, with these odd little beliefs of hers, not to mention a few peculiar old-fashioned remedies for various ailments and the odd spell or two, she would have been in trouble with the Witchfinder General.

Take warts for instance.

For as long as I could remember people had been coming to mother to get them cured.

When the best of the medical profession had failed with their antibiotics, creams and cauterising needles, mum would make those warts vanish in a few days by dabbing the afflicted part with the juice squeezed from the stem of some wild flower she found growing in the hedgerow.

Then there were the tea leaves.

There was a time when the neighbours, the women that is, were always popping in for a cuppa. Not so much for the tea (my mother made awful tea) but to get their tea leaves read.

I'd watch it all.

Drink the tea.

Leave a few dregs in the cup.

Hold the cup up high above the head in one hand, lower it and swirl it round three times, counting out loud as you go.

One.

Two.

Three.

Then upend the cup in the saucer.

Leave it for a minute or two to settle and you're ready to have your fortune told.

Dab hand at it, was mother. She would carefully lift the upside-down cup and stare into it.

What an imagination!

'I see a letter coming tomorrow. No. Perhaps the day after'.

The gas bill, as like as not.

'There's news coming from someone whose name begins with "N" . I see an "N" very clearly here. Do you know anyone whose name begins with "N"'.

Who doesn't?

'You're going on a journey quite soon. Be prepared for a journey'.

That would probably be a cycle ride to the village shop.

What a performance.

Once she grew a seedling from an apple pip which she had planted in a little pot on the window sill.

She was always experimenting with growing things in little pots, geranium cuttings, tomato seeds, holly berries and the like.

In fact the kitchen window sill was invariably crammed with an assortment of pots and jars with strange looking growths protruding from their tops.

I laughed at the apple seedling.

I told her you couldn't grow apple trees that way. They had to be grafted or something.

But she wouldn't be put off. Tended that spindly little thing like it was a baby and eventually it was big enough to be planted outside in the garden border.

By this time she'd even forgotten what sort of apple she'd started with.

About ten years must have passed and all the while that sapling grew and grew. I used to tease her about it.

Peculiar looking specimen it was with sort of spiky branches and bright green, unnatural looking leaves. More like an overgrown gooseberry bush.

Never once did it blossom.

'I see your tree hasn't flowered AGAIN this year,' I taunted one Spring.

That did it.

Next time I passed the tree I noticed there was an apple in a plastic bag hanging from one of the branches.

'What's the idea of that, then,' I wanted to know. 'Feeding the birds now are we?'

She looked at me with a scornful eye. Informed me that there was an old country saying (I'd never heard of it) that a fruitless tree could be brought into production if you could keep an apple hanging from its branches for a year and a day.

In days of old, when these old country sayings were first said, it must have been well-nigh impossible to accomplish such a feat. I ventured to suggest that wrapping an apple in a plastic bag seemed a little contrary to the spirit of the spell.

Ought to be just hung up on a string, I said.

'That's as may be,' she retorted loftily. 'But whoever it was made up this spell didn't know about plastic bags, did they? So there's nothing to say I shouldn't use one. Anyway, it'll keep the birds off'.

I told her she was going potty in her old age.

The following spring that tree was covered in blossom, produced a good crop of apples into the bargain and has done so ever since.

My mother, for one, believed it was more than just coincidence. And I, for two, am reluctantly inclined to agree.

Once she had a bit of a row with the caretaker fellow at the clubhouse where the pensioners of the village meet up every week.

It started off as a bit of a pointed remark about how they all hung about chatting when their afternoon meeting was over, when he wanted to lock up and get off home for his tea.

One thing led to another and they finished up having a proper up-and-downer.

The following week, while the meeting was in progress, she slipped away, found one of his gloves and said a few nasty words over it 'just to teach him a lesson'.

I told her she'd have the law on her if she didn't watch out.

Three days later that man went down with a nasty dose of 'flu.

Still, she must have been losing her touch.

A few years earlier he'd have been lucky to get away with a broken leg.

How she did it was a mystery to me but then the countryside is full of inexplicable phenomena.

One such I know of concerns a grave that's to be found in a bluebell wood just a few yards off the pretty little lane that runs through one of the most attractive corners of Hampshire.

Although it's only a simple, moss-covered mound with a tiny, unmarked headstone and a rough, wooden cross, the grave is still carefully tended by unknown visitors who have made regular pilgrimages to the spot for some generations past.

Yet no-one has ever seen those responsible for the work.

Every so often the locals find that the silent visitors have been in the night to clear away the weeds and undergrowth and to place fresh flowers or wild grasses and berries on the grave.

By all accounts this has been going on since the turn of the nineteenth century—back to Queen Victoria's time!

It was nearly forty years ago now that I asked one of the oldest residents of the nearby village what he knew about it.

He was himself then well into his eighties and he had known about the grave—and the mystery of the midnight pilgrims—since he was a lad. But he was just as puzzled as I was.

Sometimes the crude hazel cross had been replaced by a new one. Frequently daffodils, tulips or chrysanthemums, depending on the season, had been carefully arranged in the little vase on the grave.

Ask around the village and you can hear a number of vague and differing stories concerning the grave and its origin.

The one thing that all the yarns have in common is that a gypsy lies buried in the glade, miles from the nearest church. And they all agree that death came in violent circumstances.

One legend, for so it has now become, is that a young gypsy boy stole a diamond ring from the farm house on the hill. He was discovered and tried by a hastily convened "court" of gypsy elders, found guilty and hanged from the nearest tree.

Afterwards this Romany court decreed that his body be not burnt, as was then the gypsy custom, but that he be buried in unhallowed ground near the scene of his crime to complete his dishonour.

Another story has it that a gypsy lad fell in love with a local girl and they would meet secretly in the bluebell wood.

That is, until the girl's parents discovered their attachment.

Infuriated and disgusted, the angry parents, from a local farming family it is said, warned the gypsy off.

For good measure they packed off their erring daughter to relatives many miles away until she had forgotten her foolishness.

Meanwhile the gypsy, heartbroken at the loss of his love, hanged himself at their secret meeting place and was buried beneath the branches of the tree on which he had died.

Yet a third and more gruesome version of the story tells how a violently jealous gypsy husband, discovering his wife's infidelity with a local farmer, buried the poor woman alive, an action doubtless contrived to cure the waywardness of that unfortunate creature permanently.

All the stories involve gypsies and farmers but the real truth is now unlikely ever to be known, unless the gypsies themselves shed some light on the mystery.

I did once try questioning an old "travelling woman" who came calling at the house selling home-made clothes pegs and paper flowers (takes you back a bit!).

She was tight-lipped as she assured me: 'I don't know nuthin' about that, sur'.

If she did, she certainly wasn't telling.

Further evidence of the macabre nature of this unique burial place came to me from a former police officer. He was an extremely level-headed sort of chap—as most coppers are—and was, for a several years, the local "beat" bobby in the area which included this particular piece of countryside.

When I spoke to him he was the manager of a motor accessories shop, a keen amateur mechanic and a weekend rally driver. Hardly the type given to wild imaginings of the mind.

On top of that he was a jocular fellow with a ready wit and a stream of repartee.

But once you got him talking about the gypsy grave his face immediately took on a set and serious look.

Many's the night, while on his country beat, that he had to cycle that lonely road, pedalling his bike up the slight hill that winds through a natural avenue of magnificent beeches.

He said that, even on a warm summer night, he could feel a slight chill envelop him as he came up the hill.

The sensation of cold and damp increased with every yard as he approached that section of the road opposite the site of the grave.

And, he says, he used to experience this sensation even before he came to know that the grave existed.

It built up over a distance of several hundred yards and, ultimately, he could feel the hair bristling at the back of his neck.

'On some nights it was about as much as I could do to force myself to cycle up that hill,' he told me. 'When I did have to go that way, I really got my head down and my legs moving'.

This was the self confession of a large-sized country copper, used to dealing with belligerent drunks, runaway cattle and feuding neighbours!

'Strangely enough, as soon as you passed the spot where the grave is, the sensation ended abruptly,' he said.

'But going the other way, the exact reverse happened. You suddenly hit this cloud of fearful clamminess at the top of the hill near the grave and it gradually tapered off, diminishing as you went down the hill. It finally petered out on the level ground further down'.

This man experienced the same feeling on very many occasions, always at night.

'Sometimes it was so strong the atmosphere was almost tangible,' he said.

'At other times the sensation was barely perceptible. Often there was no sensation at all'.

He had no explanation for it.

Except that there is a mysterious presence of some extraordinary force in the vicinity of the gypsy grave.

I don't exactly believe in ghosts because I've never actually seen one. But I don't disbelieve either—and there are an awful lot of other people I know who are just as undecided.

But I'm getting way ahead of myself.

There's a whole chapter I haven't touched upon, those activities that took place in, or generated from, that amazing phenomenon known as the local youth club.

Practically every town and village in the county had one and it was the starting point for many adventures in life.

15: HITTING THE HIGH NOTES.

THE village had had a thriving youth club for years but in spite of its title you actually had to be old enough to join—you needed to be at least 13 years old—I couldn't wait!

At a time when only a very few families, the better off ones, possessed a television set, young people flocked to the slightly decrepit wooden building in the corner of the Recreation Ground on several nights a week to engage in such delights as table tennis, draughts, darts and listening to gramophone records.

The record player was a wind-up thing on which you had to renew the needle every so often to listen to people like The Platters, Roy Rogers and, later on, Frankie Laine and Johnny Ray on 78 rpm discs which shattered into pieces if dropped on the floor. And they often did.

For some time after I joined the youth club I engrossed myself each evening in one or more of the above mentioned pastimes.

Then it gradually dawned on me that there were girls of my own age there who seemed just as keen to engross themselves with me. And, to be fair, any of the other lads who wished to be so engrossed!

So it was that at the age of about 15 (I was a very late starter) I agreed to join the club's National Dancing section.

This involved regular weekly practice, to records on that same old gramophone, in such dances as Circassian Circle and Strip the Willow. It also meant giving exhibitions in front of real audiences at village fairs and fetes and church garden parties throughout the locality.

It also meant that you had an excuse for having your arm around a girl's waist!

Because, so odd as it may now seem, although I'm sure the same urges existed then as they do now, it just wasn't acceptable to be seen consorting with members of the opposite sex to such an extent as now appears the norm at ages eleven and upwards!

In any case, there wasn't the time. In summer we were too engrossed with cricket and tennis. In winter football seemed to take up most of our spare moments.

Then along came skiffle.

Way back in the earlier days of the 20th Century, before we were born, amateur musical entertainment consisted of, dare I say the word, 'nigger' minstrel groups or barber's shop quartets, quintets or sextets, depending on the number of singers.

Since those days there seemed little in the way of DIY music. Ever since the war (WWII that is) musical enjoyment was centred around 'olde tyme', or later, ballroom dancing, with nationally known 'big bands' with their resident singers being very much in vogue.

Skiffle changed all that.

It seemed to evolve from 'fill-in' periods for the big bands when three or four of the musicians would perform ad-lib acts, playing and singing old folk or western numbers and generally amusing themselves while the rest of the orchestra took a break.

Soon little groups were springing up throughout the country, especially among the younger generation.

Every secondary school, youth club, scout troop and coffee bar—a favourite haunt of youngsters at that time—seemed to boast at least one skiffle group. Some supported two, three, or even more. Our own village youth club had two groups.

It was a craze which spread with amazing rapidity until there were quite literally thousands of skiffle groups strumming and screeching all over Britain.

My own group started with ten or a dozen teenage guys armed with a wide variety of instruments, bought, borrowed or home-made, pounding out the early skiffle classics—for by now those first small professional groups were making their own records.

Lonnie Donnegan, Chas McDevitt, Nancy Whiskey, The Vipers, The Blue Grass Boys. All became almost overnight sensations.

And we all wanted to do the same.

We had about eight guitars between us, a mandolin, a banjo with only three strings, a home-made tea chest bass and a guy who proved to be totally ace on washboard and thimbles.

Nobody could play a note. Well, nobody could play a chord anyway. Nobody knew how to tune their instrument and no-one had any idea about beat or timing.

So we commandeered a large area of floor space in the youth club hut every night, stood in a circle, and bashed away. Most of us knew the words of our, then few, favourite numbers and there were new ones being broadcast all the time. So we all sang with gusto, accompanying ourselves on this vast array of instruments.

I say accompanying!

The noise was unbelievable!

What a din!

Completely out of tune and with no knowledge of the very basic chord patterns we soldiered on.

For a while.

Not surprisingly four or five of the lads got cheesed off after the first week or so and gave it up.

Then a local man, he was actually our recreation ground groundsman, who had probably heard the din each evening from his flat above the cricket pavilion, offered to help.

He could play the ukelele and explained that what we needed first was to tune our guitars and things correctly. Then we had to learn, at first, three basic chord patterns (he drew little 'window' pictures to show where we should put our fingers) and finally, to change chords at the right time in the tune.

After another couple of weeks hard practice, during which time two or three more would-be pop stars deserted the skiffle ship, we actually managed one evening, albeit in extra slow-time, to produce a sound which was recognisable as a reasonably in-tune accompaniment for one of the latest numbers to hit the skiffle charts, *'Ham 'n Eggs'*.

We were thrilled.

We practised it again.

And again.

And again.

Night after night we practised it.

Whenever we struck up the opening chord other members of the club would groan.

'Not *that* again'.

'Put a sock in it'.

'Try something else'.

'SHADDAP'.

We pressed on. After another week we tried another number, *'Worried Man Blues'*.

A week later *'Jack of Diamonds'*. Suddenly it was coming together and we could now actually perform three songs which, although not exactly professional in quality, were, nevertheless, not an assault on the ear.

A further month down the line and we had a repertoire of a dozen or more numbers.

At this point a few things need explaining for those who, amazingly, might not have heard of skiffle.

The beauty of skiffle was that a group of totally unmusical, untalented people could, with a certain amount of practice, actually make music. Their own music. And the more you practised the better you got.

We honed our own group down to five members, three guitars, a string bass and a washboard.

The guitars are, of course, self explanatory. They were all bought or otherwise acquired by the players. It was a time when guitar sales of all qualities must have reached an all-time peak in the local music shops.

So then we come to the string bass.

In its simplest form this was an empty tea chest, turned upsidedown, a hole drilled in the bottom (which then became the top) and a thick nylon string pushed through the hole and secured inside by being tied to a stick to stop it slipping back out. The other end was passed over the top of a broom head and fixed to the handle.

The bottom of the handle (with the string adjusted for length) was placed on the top (bottom) of the tea chest and by pulling the broom handle back and forth the tension on the string was altered—changing the note of this primitive bass instrument. It made a terrific, deep thumping sound.

Our own bass had moved on very slightly from the broom handle phase. It had a stout two-by-one inch spar fixed securely (that means screwed) to the side of the tea chest to the top of which the nylon bass string was permanently fixed.

Mike, our bass player, could then alter the note of the bass by sliding his fingers up and down this primitive keyboard like a real bass player, although the choice of note was pretty limited.

But it was the thump, thump, thump of the tea chest bass which kept us all in time.

Then there was that other skiffle necessity, the washboard.

This was bought from the local ironmongers shop in Basingstoke. It was a rectangular piece of rigid, corrugated galvanised iron with a wooden frame, about two feet by one foot (700m x 350m).

It was meant for scrubbing the washing on and, remarkably, in those days before washing machines, was still in use in a few households. I doubt if it is available today.

The washboard 'player', Dick in our case, then placed a metal thimble on the end of each finger and, seated with the washboard across his knees, strummed the thing back and forth in time to produce a sound not unlike that of a kettle drum.

Our three guitars were handled by myself, Brian and Tony.

Every skiffle group had to have an impressive name, even the out and out amateur ones like ours.

What should ours be?

We argued and pondered for ages.

By this time the other members of the youth club, totally fed up with our nightly cacophony, had politely asked us to practise somewhere else. Come to think of it the requests, which became louder, more frequent and considerably more forceful as time went on, weren't all that polite either!

So one Wednesday evening when the pub across the road was particularly lacking in customers, we were sitting in their otherwise deserted and grandly named 'saloon bar' bemoaning our lack of rehearsal room and sipping our halves of whatever (remember we were in our late 'teens by now) when kindly landlady Linda said: 'Why don't you practise in here? We're always quiet on a Wednesday.'

That's how Wednesday night became our rehearsal night at the Bolton Arms. Although, it must be said, we had no idea what we were rehearsing for!

And, do you know, people started looking through from the 'Jug and Bottle' snug bar next door and even customers in the ever-popular 'Public' at the other end of the building began standing at the doorway and tapping their feet.

So it was that we named ourselves *The Innsiders*.

Very nearly.

Except that we couldn't agree on how to spell it. Should it be *InnSIDERS, InnCIDERS,* or even *InnCYDERS*?

Eventually we dropped the idea and as there was currently a popular strong bottled beer called Five X, and there were, after all, five of us, we kind of slipped into calling ourselves *The Five Xs*.

It was more a name by default than a carefully planned public relations decision.

But *The Five Xs* we became and *The Five Xs* we remained throughout our relatively short playing career.

Moving into the pub had definite advantages.

For one thing we began to get an audience, which improved our confidence and boosted our egos.

At first just a handful of listeners, usually our girl friends and fans from the youth club, filling a few seats in the normally empty Saloon Bar.

Then, as our repertoire expanded and our presentation became more (much more) acceptable, the odd visitors who did drop in casually on our rehearsal nights, made planned return trips. And they brought their friends.

Within a month or two Wednesday night at the Bolton Arms at Old Basing was no longer a quiet midweek evening.

People came in their dozens, some from many miles away, to listen to this new live skiffle group. And it has to be said that landlady Linda was delighted with this new and unexpected leap in her Wednesday night takings.

At times the Saloon Bar was so packed there was hardly room for the band!

And naturally everyone who came to watch and listen to these five young guys making some kind of music on their improvised instruments, wanted to buy us all a drink.

'Get one in for the boys', we would hear several times a night. And another five full glasses would appear on the little square table set aside especially for that purpose.

After the first few weeks none of us ever had to pay for a drink throughout Wednesday evening.

One would have thought we would have been staggering by closing time but in fact we were so busy playing and singing we hardly had time to drink!

Three or four halves would last us all evening and, remember, licensed closing time was either ten o'clock or half past ten in those days.

Our popularity was in part due to the fact that country pubs offered very little in the way of entertainment at that time. Very few served food, in fact pub meals were virtually unknown. A packet of Smith's crisps (just the one 'potato' flavour with the salt in a little bit of twisted blue paper) and a bag of peanuts was about all you could expect, although a few (not the Bolton Arms) did offer a simple 'ploughman's lunch of cheese, bread and pickle at midday on a Saturday.

Television was still for the relatively few. A pub with live entertainment in the middle of the week was something of a novelty and people had a little more money in their pockets than in the immediate post-war days. They wanted to spend it. A trip out to listen to a skiffle group was just what the doctor ordered.

Then came the talent competitions.

At first we had to be badgered and cajoled into entering a contest that was being held in the cinema of a small town six or seven miles away.

It was a late night affair and was scheduled to follow the main film showing that night. I can't remember what it was called or what it was about except that it starred Peter Finch and Mary Urr. The thing was that, although we actually got free admission to the cinema, we were too tense, while waiting for our turn to appear on stage, to take much notice of the screen.

We had brought along a dozen or more of our faithful supporters and as the competition was to be judged on audience response—and our lot could be pretty noisy—we were quietly confident of lifting first prize of a few quid which was worth quite a lot in those days.

We reckoned without the Air Force.

Less than a mile from the cinema was a big RAF station (there still is) and at least half the audience was made up by personnel from the camp.

Our turn came and on stage we went.

Our first real public appearance in front of a critical audience.

Were we nervous?

I know I was!

We broke into our favourite *Jack 'o Diamonds* and followed it up with *Worried Man Blues*. We were great.

The audience loved it and gave us a terrific round of applause.

Trouble was that some attractive young female singer with a rather fetching figure came on and seemed to tickle the fancy of the scores of airmen in the place.

They nearly brought the roof down.

I'm not suggesting for a minute that she couldn't sing. She was quite good.

But not as good as us.

We ended up with second prize, a fact that we ever after blamed on the men of the local Air Force base!

But that was just the start.

As our reputation grew so did the invitations to play at various venues around the area. We found a number of local pubs wanted us to perform for their Friday and Saturday night clientele.

And they were willing to pay!

We continued to play our regular Wednesday night spot at the Bolton Arms free of charge and customers continued to crowd in.

Our wealthy local youth club benefactor treated us to a 'uniform' of our choice—bright yellow shirts and bright blue jeans. Pub landlady Linda bought us all pretty fetching blue cravats.

Did we ever look cool!

Our next problem was what to charge for an evening's performance.

We settled on five pounds a night, a quid apiece. Which seemed to be fair. Mind you, at that time you could buy a lot more for your £1 than you can today.

Trying to think back to what typical prices were is difficult but I seem to recall that a gallon (not a litre!) of petrol was about half-a-crown (12p), half a pint of bottled beer was about two bob (10p), a packet of crisps was 4d (less than 2p) and you could get into the pictures (that's the cinema) for around 1/9 (about 9p).

It's quite true that with ten bob (50p) you could catch the bus into town, go to the pictures, have a fish and chip supper, catch the bus back home and still have change in your pocket!

Remember, however, that wages were just a little lower than today. My first job (on the farm) paid 50 shillings for a week's work (that's £2.50p).

Our next foray into competition playing came in the shape of our entry into the local heat of a country-wide contest held by a national daily newspaper.

There were dozens of skiffle groups anxious to show off their talents so we joined the queue.

It was held in one of the three cinemas in Basingstoke one afternoon instead of the usual matinee film performance.

We won it hands down!

We were riding high and our supporting followers grew in number.

At the next heat we were again placed first in the north Hampshire regional competition, which meant we were now qualified to play in the county finals at one of Southampton's huge cinemas.

We took a coach load of our faithful supporters with us. The auditorium, holding over a thousand people, was heaving.

And we came up against competition like never before.

Some of the groups had managers!

They came among us, trying to tell us what we could and could not play. There were, of course, just a handful of skiffle numbers riding high in the charts at the time (it was called the Hit Parade!). Someone else insisted any number had to be a genuine skiffle song.

By the time we went on stage I, for one, was shaking. We had agreed among us we'd do *Worried Man Blues*. The first group on (we were scheduled next to last at number five) played it!

Catastrophe!

We didn't want to repeat what someone else had already done so we held a quick backstage conference. We switched our choice to *Jack 'o Diamonds.*

Group number four did it!

We were on! We had no time to switch again so we did the same number. Better, I believed, than the previous group but simply repeating the same number was not exactly a vote winner.

Last group on was a group from Bournemouth (which in those days was in Hampshire, not being 'moved' into Dorset until about twenty years later).

They had a manager, a real double bass, proper drum kit and electric guitars. Their sound was far from amateur and they did a number which was about as far removed from pure skiffle as Elvis Presley from Debussy.

It was *I Wish that I could Shimmy like my Sister Kate*. And it sounded great.

They won!

Can't remember the name of the group or whether they went on to bigger things. We returned home, having got only third or fourth place and realising that, good as we were locally, we weren't really good enough to cut the mustard on the wider national stage.

Still, we were still the best for miles around and we spent the next year or so enjoying ourselves and playing in pubs around the environs of Basingstoke.

We were even booked to play for a dance in a tiny local village hall not many miles from home. We had assumed we would be supporting a main dance band but arrived to discover WE were the main dance band.

And some local tough guy kept coming up to ask for a waltz!

Anyone ever tried dancing a waltz to *Rock Island Line* ?

The organisers of this little village hop seemed quite put out when we told them we weren't able to play non-stop from 7.30pm until after midnight, and that we would require a break of a least half an hour some time during the evening.

'But what will we do?' They wailed. 'We can't just have silence for half an hour'.

'Get a gramophone'. Was our advice.

Somebody's 'Dansette' wind-up was produced along with a few records and we hastily departed to the pub just down the road.

All this hassle for five quid. We vowed there and then that we'd never make that mistake again. And we didn't.

We played, open air, in the bandstand at Basingstoke War Memorial Park and we played on stage at the Haymarket Theatre during the town's annual Carnival Week.

But the writing was on the wall.

After about two years of amazing popularity, skiffle was on the wane.

Rock and Roll became big, big time, and still is after more than five decades!

Our star quickly faded and The Five Xs disappeared, with thousands of other skiffle groups, into oblivion.

Today, as I write, 55 years on (can it really be 55 years?) four of us are still (just) in existence and still good friends. Indeed, a couple of us regularly play golf together, weather permitting and I occasionally get out my guitar and perform a little private number or two for my own amusement.

Yes, skiffle has gone.

But the memories linger on. And they are just great!

Enough of all this pulsating excitement as we turn our attention to something much more to do with the natural world.

16: THE GENTLE GIANTS.

IT was a wild night. A gale ripped through the countryside, sending dustbin lids clattering along the road and bringing tiles crashing down off the roofs.

In the calm that followed next day, I was passing one of my favourite places, the old bridge over the river, when I was horrified to see a most dramatic change in the scenery.

There was a great hole in the sky where the big silver poplar had stood. That tree had been an essential part of the beautiful riverside view for as long as I, or anyone else for that matter, could remember.

A victim of the midnight storm, the once mighty tree now lay in a pathetic confusion of broken and twisted branches, half blocking the stream.

Already men were at work with power saws, slicing it into sections for removal. A few days later all that remained to indicate that the tree had ever existed was the shattered hollow stump jutting raggedly from the river bank.

Of course, everyone knew it was hollow.

When we were smaller we could squeeze inside. And once a swarm of bees had made a home there, building masses of white comb stretching right up the inside of the great trunk and which, despite our efforts at smoking the bees out by lighting fires in the bottom, remained uncollected for years.

So it was not altogether a surprise to see that it had come down.

It was just the shock realisation that that lovely scene would never be the same again, not in our own lifetime anyway.

It was one of those marvellous round-topped poplars, not the characterless, pencil-slim Lombardy type.

It grew close by the river bridge and, although not a weeping tree, it did overhang the water, as though gazing at its own reflection, making the spot one of the most picturesque in the village.

When the poplar was in full leaf, it was capable of showing a startling change of moods. On an airless summer day it would stand silent and seemingly lifeless.

But the very slightest stirring of a breeze would send the leaves all a-tremble, showing in rapid alternation their green tops and silvery undersides, whispering faintly as they did so and giving the effect of a silver-green monster shaking his cloak at the passing clouds.

A gentle giant.

Now it's gone and I only hope that someone eventually takes it upon themselves to plant a replacement. The scene looks strangely bare without it.

The sense of loss at the fall of that old poplar reminded me of a similar sentiment experienced when they cut our favourite conker trees down.

From our cottage window I could see them, a pair of identical twin horse chestnuts. I watched them change character as the seasons progressed, year after year.

In winter they were sleeping giants, leafless, dark and sombre.

By March the brown "sticky buds", covered in a kind of resin and which would eventually produce the new growth, were well developed.

In May the pair put on a miraculous display of thousands of cream-coloured "candles" of flower, showing vividly against the new, pale green mantle of leaves and looking for all the world like enormous out-of-season Christmas trees.

Later the candles disappeared, as the green of the leaves grew darker, to be replaced by clusters of spiky-cased horse chestnuts which grew bigger and bigger as the year wore on.

In autumn the leaves turned to yellow and gold and brown and began to fall. The chestnut cases split to show glimpses of the shiny dark brown conkers inside.

Then these, too, tumbled to the ground, assisted more often than not by sticks thrown by the hordes of village children.

They were the best conkers in the district. Not surprising as the two trees were by far the largest and grandest of their species for many miles around.

I don't know just how tall those trees were but suffice it to say that I had never seen larger horse chestnut trees before. Nor have I since.

Then one night a great bough crashed down in the lane that ran close by.

No-one was hurt. No real damage done.

But what followed was, perhaps, inevitable.

The trees were inspected, declared to be unsafe, and both were felled.

I remember watching, a lump in my throat, as those magnificent specimens came crashing to earth with a thunderous roar, throwing up masses of dust and twigs and leaves, the very ground shaking with the impact.

It was a specialist who cut them down.

I think it affected him almost as much as it had us.

'The biggest I've ever seen,' he said.

He measured them.

Each was over seven feet across at the base and he estimated their age at well over two hundred years.

Two hundred years to grow—and it took about twenty minutes each to cut them down!

The man said that had they been looked at earlier they could probably have been saved for another fifty years or so. Which made me wonder: why hadn't they been looked at earlier? They, too, have never been replaced.

At least the motive for their felling was reasonably sound. Not like the thinking behind the destruction of another nice tree I knew.

An oak tree, this one, not enormous as oaks go but a fine healthy mature tree, who knows, perhaps a hundred or more years old.

It stood, not too close to the road, on a wide grassy verge and got in nobody's way.

That is, until they decided to widen the road so that the cars could go even faster.

Even then, although much closer to the carriageway, the tree didn't seem to mind the extra traffic noise, pollution and disturbance and all should have been well.

But one wet night a madcap young car driver, who later admitted having had far too much to drink, lost control of his vehicle which careered off the road, mounted the verge and crashed headlong into the great oak, killing the other three occupants, all teenage girls.

The driver got the blame, of course, but the local council decided that the tree was dangerous too.

The car driver was fined.

The tree was sentenced to death.

They cut it down, sawed it up and carted it away. The most blatant revenge killing of an innocent that I have ever witnessed.

Most of us, country folk that is, have a favourite tree. A tree that for some reason is that little bit special. Mine was an old apple tree.

It grew in our ancient cottage garden and was no recognisable type or species that I could tell.

It was very old, for an apple tree, its trunk spread into two massive limbs only a few feet from the ground, it grew lots of small green apples with russet-coloured striations which weren't noticeable for their eating qualities.

And it was very easy to climb.

Now for me an "easy" tree has to be about as difficult to climb as a staircase—and not too steep a staircase at that!

This tree was one such.

Being absolutely terrified of heights I never climbed very high. But that apple tree was at various times to me a sailing ship, a mountain, a burning building, an aircraft, a balloon and a church steeple. Not to mention my refuge from all manner of ferocious and dangerous wild beasts.

Years after we had moved, the estate to whom the cottage belonged sold it off. The new occupiers made a really grand job of renovation and extension, even using old timbers and second hand bricks to tone in with the original shell.

Only my old apple tree had to come down of course—to make way for a big new garage.

No tree has ever deliberately harmed a human being and yet for thousands of years man has used and abused the tree, one of the largest and gentlest living things on earth.

We've built our homes, our ships and our furniture from mighty trees that took many human generations to mature.

Thankfully we've sat in the leafy shade of a tree on a hot afternoon. And just as thankfully sheltered beneath its boughs on a wet one.

Its branches have been used to stoke our fires in the cold months of winter, its leaves and flowers picked to decorate and brighten our houses in spring

And it was in an oak tree that the future King Charles II found concealment from the Roundheads after losing the battle of Worcester in 1651, enabling him to fight another day and eventually regain the English crown.

The trees of pre-history spent eons processing the toxic atmosphere of this planet so that life such as our own could later develop and flourish.

All this and what is their reward?

If it suits our purpose we allow a few selected specimens to stay awhile to grace our parks and gardens. And all too often it's not long before we find that even they seem to have been planted in the wrong place and are getting in the way of "progress".

You'd think the middle of a wood was a pretty safe place for tree. How wrong can you be!

A recently completed highway scheme near here entailed the building of a new road right through the centre of one of our largest local copses.

There were a few protests but in the end the plan went through, the wood was sliced in half, hundreds of trees of all species were scythed down in a huge swathe. All so that a few more cars can go a little bit faster, get to wherever they're going a little bit sooner—and kill a few extra people (and a lot more wildlife) on the way.

Among other things, deer still use their ancient travelling paths through that woodland, in spite of the fact that their route now takes them straight across a busy new dual carriageway.

Fortunately there are some trees, in preservation areas, that with luck will see a few more hundred years of undisturbed existence.

The biggest yew tree I know is in such a place, well off the nearest road and that one only a quiet country lane.

It has a huge, gnarled trunk, twisted like a giant stick of barley sugar and divides into the most beautiful array of branches that just invites children—and not a few adults—to climb it.

I have the feeling that children will be enjoying this particular yew tree for many years to come.

Then there's an avenue of beeches I know, two rows of splendid trees which stand each side of a particularly attractive lane.

The great, smooth grey trunks go straight up like stone columns, the dark canopy overhangs the road at a considerable height and it's not difficult to imagine that you're walking up the aisle of the cathedral dedicated to the god of nature.

There's an interesting story attached to one old tree I know and it's a tree that, luckily, the local authority has pledged to preserve at all cost.

It stands beside the road leading out of a small Hampshire town.

And it has a name.

Frenchman's Oak.

It seems that during the Napoleonic wars a number of French prisoners of war were billeted in a camp constructed in a great chalk pit in the town, a story borne out by the existence of two gravestones in the burial ground of the parish church, marking the last resting place of two young internees who died in captivity.

At that time, in the early 1800s, the prisoners, mostly officers, were given considerable freedom and were allowed out of the prison camp on their word of honour that they would not try to escape.

They could wander the town itself but were allowed to go no more than a mile from the prison camp. The oak tree outside the town was even then a mature specimen and marked the boundary of their parole on one of their favourite walks.

Inevitably, especially in summer, the tree became the meeting place out of camp for many of the prisoners and must have been the unhearing, unseeing witness to countless stories from homesick Frenchmen as they sat beneath its branches trying to while away the boredom of their captivity.

That's obviously how the tree got its name.

But there's a villain of the piece in the form of the local English bully-boy.

The military authorities apparently offered a bounty of one shilling for the capture of any escaped prisoner of war.

That meant, of course, that they had to be more than a mile from the prison camp before they were deemed to have "escaped".

This enterprising fellow, whose name is not recorded, made quite a business out of collecting bounties.

He would pounce on an unsuspecting lone prisoner, out for an innocent stroll, as soon as he passed the tree, in spite of the fact that the poor man had absolutely no intention of trying to escape.

And, it is said, he on more than one occasion collared a Frenchman walking legitimately inside the boundary, dragged him up the road a few hundred yards, tied him hand and foot and then called for the militia to claim his shilling, swearing that the man had been caught in the act of running away.

This not only netted him a very valuable cash reward, it frequently left the Frenchman bruised and bloodied, landed him in trouble with the prison authorities and made all the other captives very angry.

His goose was finally cooked one evening when several of the more robust prisoners concealed themselves in the oak tree, dropping to the ground at the precise moment to catch him red-handed in the act of "pressing" yet another of their unfortunate colleagues.

They seized him, carried him shoulder high up the road to the newly-opened canal, and heaved him off the parapet of the bridge into the water.

So ended his "nice little earner" and he never tried his trick again.

The oak, which must now be something like 300 years old, still stands. The great trunk has at various times been lopped, the branches trimmed and smeared over with anti-rot fluid to stop disease getting in.

Its largest limb, an enormous bough, juts out from the shortened trunk at right angles and had grown so long and heavy over the years that it has had to be supported by a hefty timber prop to stop it pulling the whole tree over.

Frenchman's Oak is old. Very old. But it is still alive. And what's more important, is enjoying in its old age the most expert attention available.

Not like the lime tree outside the village school.

It is a young tree—as trees go—planted in 1935 to commemorate the Silver Jubilee of King George V. But already it's suffered the effects of man's thoughtlessness.

When it was planted the village elders had a nice little circular iron seat erected around the base of the sapling, so that in later years people could sit comfortably in its shade.

Trouble was, they forgot to allow for the tree to grow outwards as well as upwards and for years the metal band of the seat was cutting irresistibly into the bark of the expanding trunk.

Thankfully the old iron seat has now been replaced by a larger, wooden one.

But they've had to lop the top out of the tree to accommodate an electricity cable which passes directly overhead.

Whether the tree was planted right under the cable or whether the cable was erected right over the young tree I don't know.

Either way it showed an amazing lack of foresight on someone's part!

There were trees on this earth long before man's ancestors had managed to drag themselves out of the primeval slime and I've no doubt there will be trees here long after the human race has succeeded in its senseless headlong scurry for self extinction.

An awareness of nature is, thankfully, beginning to emerge. Unfortunately, in the case of trees it has taken such phenomena as Dutch elm disease and an English hurricane to bring this about.

Even now, although it is too late for the thousands of splendid elms of the English countryside, there is hope for many other species.

All it takes is a little thought, a little time and a little respect and man could be enjoying the beauty and reaping the benefits of trees—and host of other natural wonders—for centuries to come.

I do hope so.

But enough of this maudlin sentimentality!

Soon there were to be other, more pleasant subjects to attract my attention.

Printed in Great
Britain
by Amazon